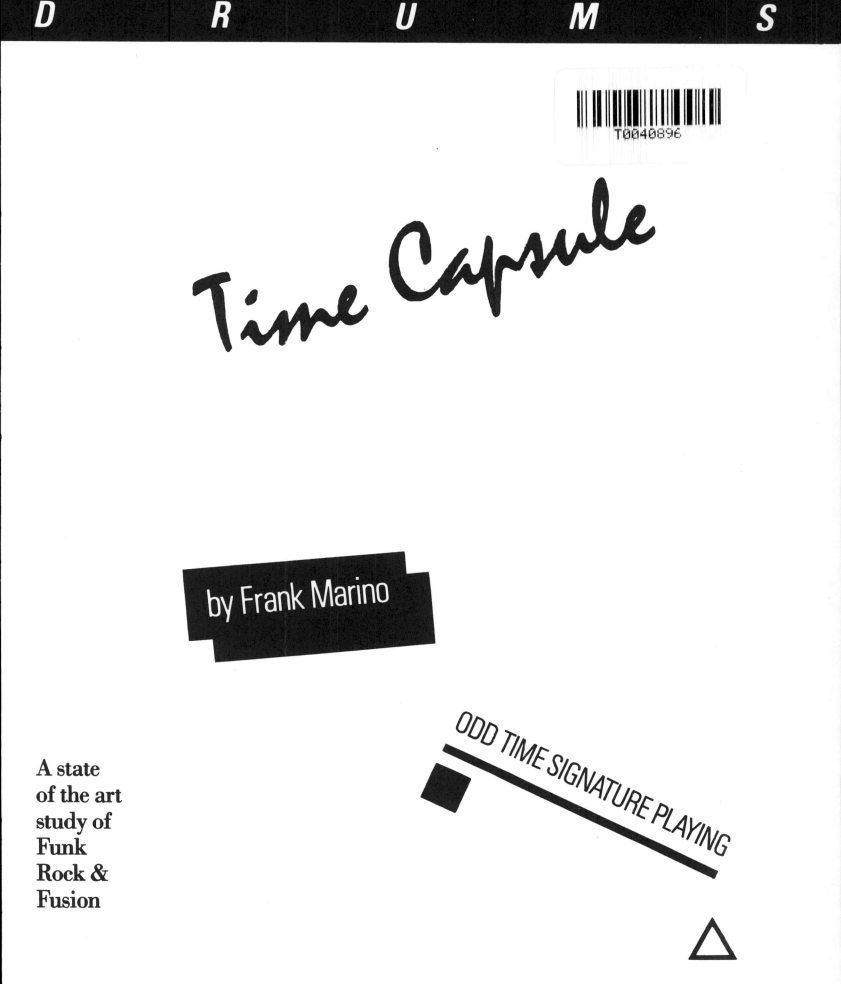

Time Capsule

by Frank Marino

A state
of the art
study of
Funk
Rock &
Fusion

ODD TIME SIGNATURE PLAYING

dc publications

Distributed by

Hal Leonard Publishing Corporation

7777 West Bluemound Road   P.O. Box 13819   Milwaukee, Wisconsin 53213

T0040896

DOM FAMULARO — Editorial Consultant

PETER MICHAEL MARINO — Cover Design

TONY GALLINO — Musical Copyist

I would especially like to thank **Dom Famularo,** *a sincere and dedicated artist, for giving so much of himself to this book both conceptually as well as creatively.*

And Jerry Ricci, for his constant support and encouragement.

ACKNOWLEDGMENTS

To Christine and Guy for their true inspiration and help. My brothers Peter, Paul and Jess, whose love and support defines brotherhood. Charlie Roeder and Chet Doboe for giving me the confidence. Tony Gallino for doing such a great job. Al Miller, Dennis Ricci, Kent Lewis, and Barry Kripitzer for their support. To all of my students over the years for their input. And of course my dear mother for caring so very much and my father for "bustin' my chops". I thank God for all your help and Him for His. This book is sincerely dedicated to each of you.

1ST PRINTING 1983

2ND PRINTING 1992

D.C. Publications 2489 Charles Court, North Bellmore, NY 11710

TABLE OF CONTENTS

PAGE #

INTRODUCTION 2

IMPORTANT PERFORMANCE NOTES and KEY TO DRUM NOTATION 3, 4, 5

PRELIMINARY EXERCISES IN 7/8 . . . . 6, 7

MUSICAL EXAMPLE NO. 1 . . . . 8, 9

MUSICAL EXAMPLE NO. 2 . . . . 10, 11

MUSICAL EXAMPLE NO. 3 12

PRELIMINARY EXERCISES IN 9/8 . . . . 13, 14

MUSICAL EXAMPLE NO. 4 15

MUSICAL EXAMPLE NO. 5 . . . . 16, 17

MUSICAL EXAMPLE NO. 6 . . . . 18, 19

PRELIMINARY EXERCISES IN 11/8 . . . . 20, 21

MUSICAL EXAMPLE NO. 7 . . . . 22, 23

PRELIMINARY EXERCISES IN 5/8 . . . . 24, 25

MUSICAL EXAMPLE NO. 8 . . . . 26, 27

PRELIMINARY EXERCISES IN 6/8 . . . . 28, 29

MUSICAL EXAMPLE NO. 9 . . . . 30, 31

MUSICAL EXAMPLE NO. 10 32

PRELIMINARY EXERCISES IN 19/8 . . . . 33, 34, 35

MUSICAL EXAMPLE NO. 11 . . . . 36, 37, 38

PRELIMINARY EXERCISES IN 20/8 . . . . 39, 40

MUSICAL EXAMPLE NO. 12 41

MUSICAL EXAMPLE NO. 13 42

PRELIMINARY EXERCISES IN 3/4 and 5/4 . . . . 43, 44

MUSICAL EXAMPLE NO. 14 45

MUSICAL EXAMPLE NO. 15 . . . . 46, 47

PRELIMINARY EXERCISES IN 6/4 . . . . 48, 49

MUSICAL EXAMPLE NO. 16 . . . . 50, 51, 52, 53

MUSICAL EXAMPLE NO. 17 AND 18 54

PRELIMINARY EXERCISES IN 7/4 . . . . 55, 56

MUSICAL EXAMPLE NO. 19 57

MUSICAL EXAMPLE NO. 20 . . . . 58, 59

PRELIMINARY EXERCISES IN 4/4 PLUS 6/8 60

MUSICAL EXAMPLE NO. 21 . . . . 61, 62

PRELIMINARY EXERCISES IN 7/8 PLUS 4/4 63

MUSICAL EXAMPLE NO. 22 . . . . 64, 65

PHRASING ODD METERS WITHIN A 4/4 TIME STRUCTURE 66, 67

MUSICAL EXAMPLE NO. 23 AND 24 68

MUSICAL EXAMPLE NO. 25 69

MUSICAL EXAMPLE NO. 26 70

AMETRIC STUDIES, MUSICAL EXAMPLE NO. 27 71

MUSICAL EXAMPLE NO. 28, 29 72

MUSICAL EXAMPLE NO. 30 73

INTRODUCTION

Odd time signatures are becoming increasingly more commonplace in contemporary music. Today's drummer is not only expected to be able to play musically in 3/4, 4/4 and 6/8 time, but also to create interesting patterns in time signatures such as 7/8, 9/8 and 11/8 to name a few. It is important that the drummer not be mechanical in his playing so that the rhythms can flow and sound natural.

In compiling this work, it was my intention to introduce the reader to various ways of playing unusual time signatures which are being used in today's popular Rock, Funk and Fusion drumming. The use of ("odd") time signatures has crossed over from Indian, Greek, African and many other ethnic influences to today's drumset player. Creative musicians are always looking for new avenues of expression. Composers have only just begun to tap the rich resources that different and interesting time signatures present in all styles of music. I feel that it is essential for you to fully comprehend what has already been accomplished by other drummers in order to understand where the state of the art is now, and then to hopefully take it to an even higher level. As great as some drummers' contributions have been to date, most drumset players are still in their infancy as far as the possibilities that different time signatures present.

The truly inspiring drummers, whose work I found essential to study, provide a fair assessment of contemporary Rock, Funk and Fusion time signature playing. These artists include Terry Bozzio, Gerry Brown, Bill Bruford, Mike Clark , Billy Cobham, Phil Collins, Jack DeJohnette, Steve Gadd, Ed Greene, Curt Kress, Harvey Mason, Alphonse Mouzon, Neil Peart, Simon Phillips, Narada Michael Walden, Lenny White and Tony Williams, as well as many other great musicians who have influenced me.

It has become evident that in order for a drummer to have a well rounded musical education, he must be versed in odd time signatures. They are not something that you should practice only when you have some extra time on your hands, but an integral part of the study of drums. Remember, "people tend to be down on what they are not up on." So, if you have downplayed the importance of studying odd time signatures, it may be that you haven't yet been exposed to them or realize their value. Hopefully, this book will be a step in the right direction.

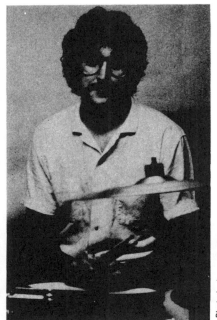

Photo by Laura A. Malone

Frank Marino

©

IMPORTANT PERFORMANCE NOTES

KEY TO DRUM NOTATION

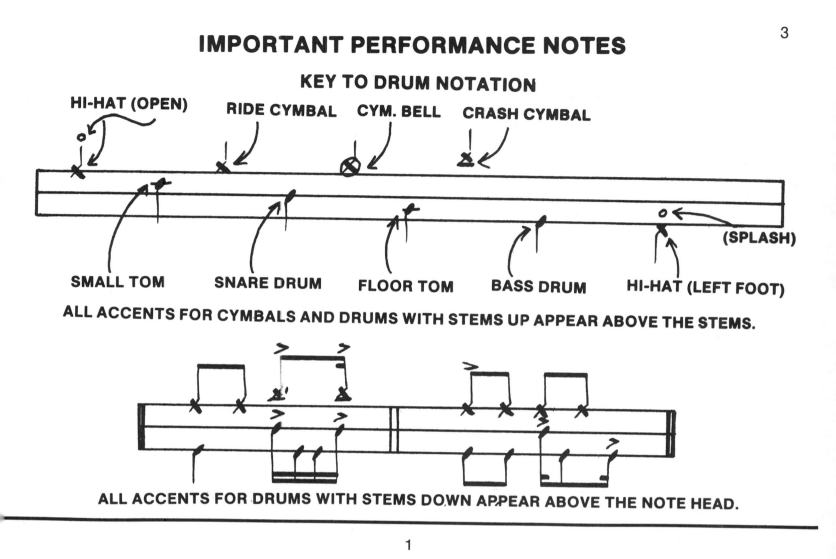

ALL ACCENTS FOR CYMBALS AND DRUMS WITH STEMS UP APPEAR ABOVE THE STEMS.

ALL ACCENTS FOR DRUMS WITH STEMS DOWN APPEAR ABOVE THE NOTE HEAD.

1

In contemporary music, meter change may also involve a change in pulse. For example, a 2/4 measure may be followed by a measure of 3/8 time.

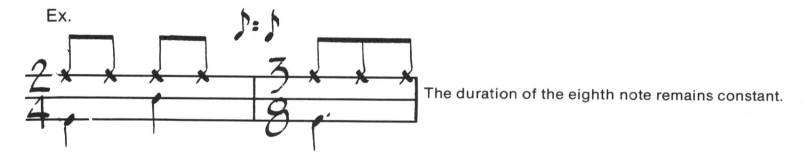

The duration of the eighth note remains constant.

Quarter note pulse can also be followed by sixteenth note pulse.

The speed of the sixteenth note remains constant.

Ex.

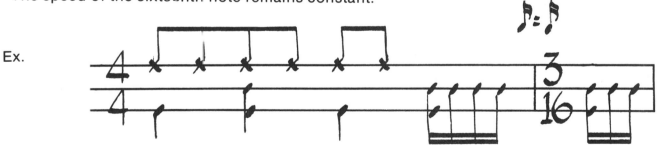

To help you understand the rhythms presented in this text I will break down the time signatures into shorter patterns. For example, 7/8 time might be described as 2/4 plus 3/8 or 3/4 plus 1/8, however, technically it is 7/8 time being broken down. I am merely using this as a method of explanation. Once you feel comfortable with this concept, you should try to feel the rhythm in an even pulse of seven.

©

One suggested method for practicing the rhythms contained in the preliminary exercise sections is to use what I term a "modular approach". For example, first learn one segment of a 7/8 rhythm.

Then practice the next part individually.

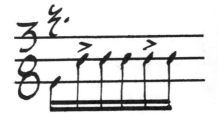

And finally group them together.

It is common to describe this rhythm as 4/8 plus 3/8. The reason I use 2/4 plus 3/8 is to make it clearer to the majority of drummers who seem to have a better working knowledge of quarter note based time signatures than eighth note time signatures and therefore this would make the modular approach more understandable. This technique is effective because it pieces two familiar concepts together to help you understand and create more involved patterns. Many additional exercises can be constructed simply by interchanging parts with other examples of the same breakdown. It is suggested that you use whichever method of counting that you're most comfortable with.

3

Whenever the ride cymbal is being played the hi-hat foot should play the pulse. In 5/4 rhythm the hi-hat plays 5 quarter notes.

In a 9/8 rhythm the hi-hat plays 9 eighth notes.

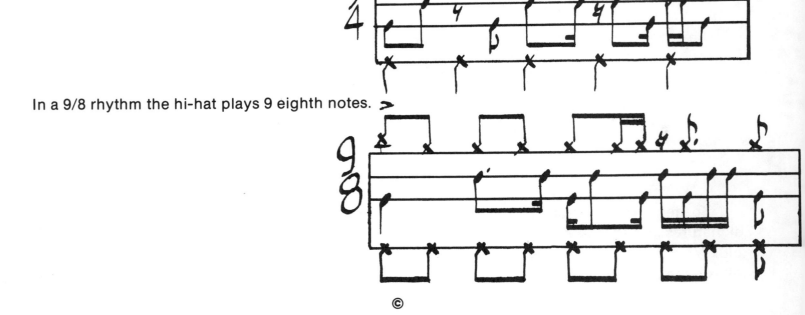

4

The breakdowns used in this text apply directly to the musical examples. There are as many breakdowns of a time signature as are mathematically possible. For example, 9 can be broken down into 6 + 3, 7 + 2, 5 + 4, etc. However, the examples chosen suggest some of the more practical applications relating to Rock, Funk and Fusion drumming. There are other musical ways to breakdown time signatures. It is suggested that you experiment with different breakdowns and listen to a wide variety of music containing odd time signatures.

5

The musical examples in this text contain some suggested accent markings. It is important to learn these first and then experiment with some of your own. Try to avoid the very common "boxed in" sound that results from a loud accent on the first beat of each measure. Be very aware of how you accent, because accents have a significant effect on the flow of these rhythms

6

The time signatures presented here can be studied in a different order. You may want to begin with the time signature that *you* are the most comfortable with and then proceed in the order of difficulty that each meter presents to you. Keep in mind that you should complete each preliminary exercise section before moving to the next time signature.

7

The reader should explore the different tonal possibilities of the rhythms.

Original rhythm

Suggested Variations

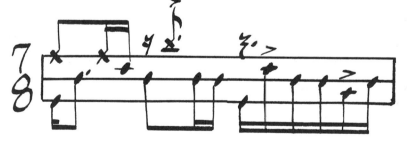

Also experiment by applying the rhythms to Double Bass Drums, Roto-toms, electronic percussion, etc...(the possibilities are infinite.)

PRELIMINARY EXERCISES IN $\frac{7}{8}$

These exercises are designed to demonstrate the technique of breaking down a measure of 7/8 time into one bar of 3/4 time, plus one-eighth note. This gives the rhythm the feeling of an abbreviated measure of 4/4, which can also be thought of as 3½/4.

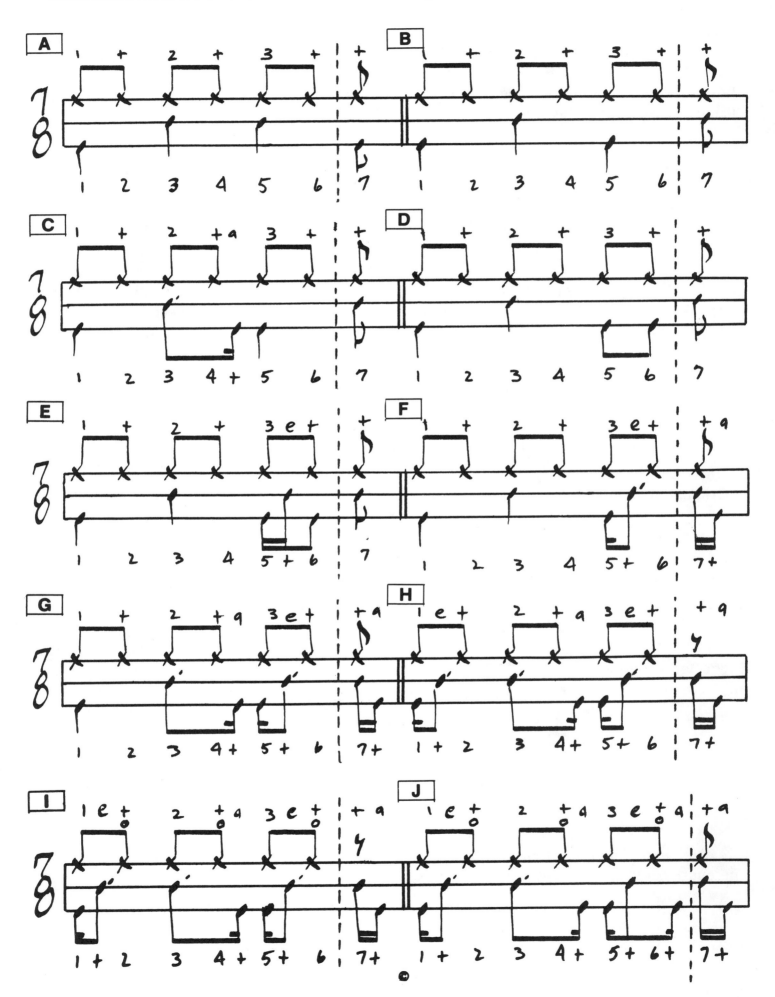

In this 7/8 exercise, the 2/4 measure comes first, and the measure of 3/8 follows.

These are examples of subdividing 7/8 time into a 3/8 measure followed by a bar of 2/4.

MUSICAL EXAMPLE NO. 1

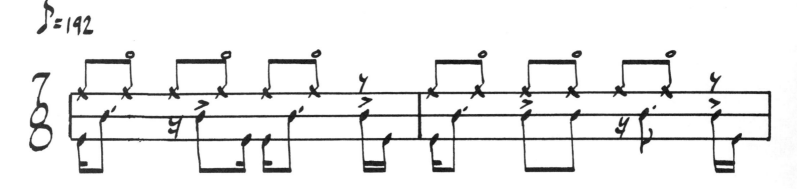

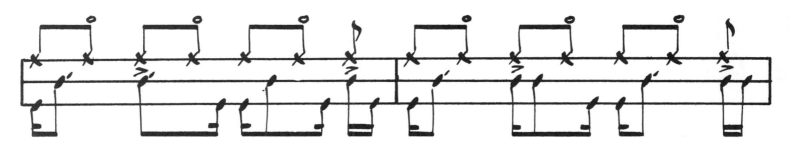

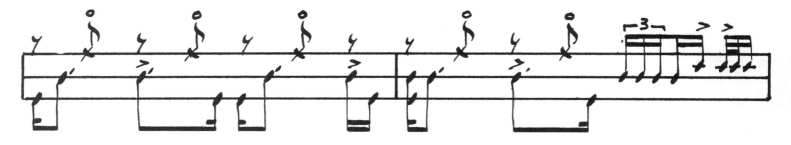

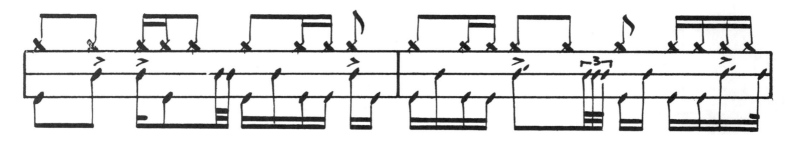

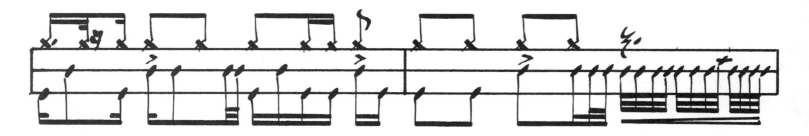

©

MUSICAL EXAMPLE CONTINUED...

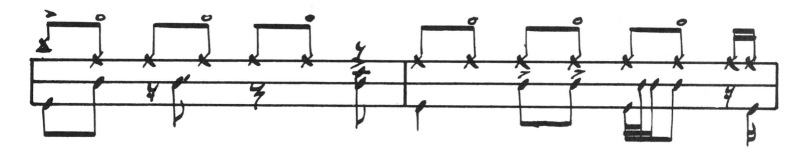

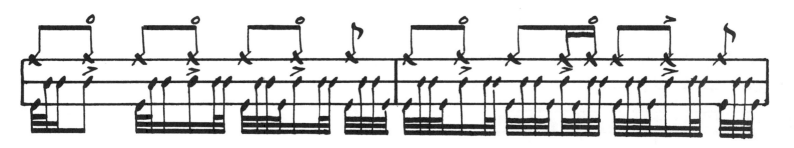

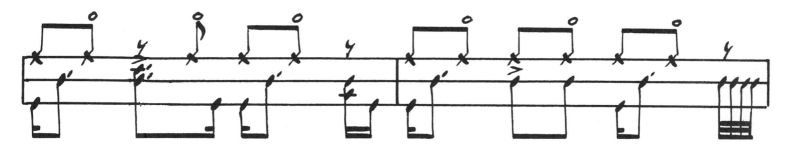

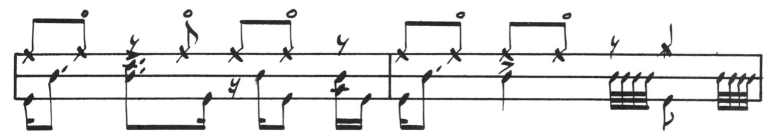

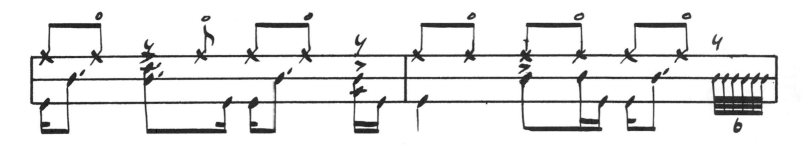

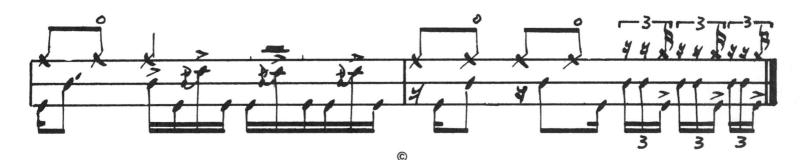

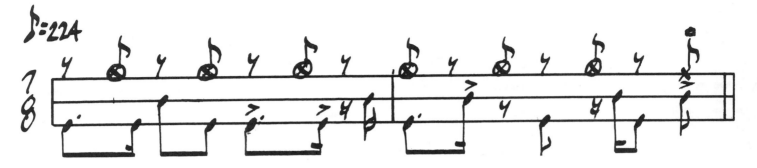

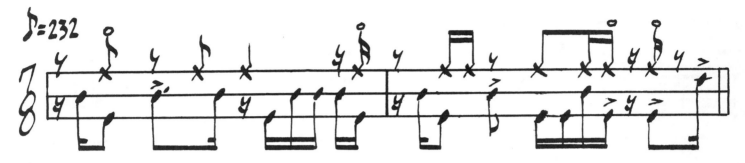

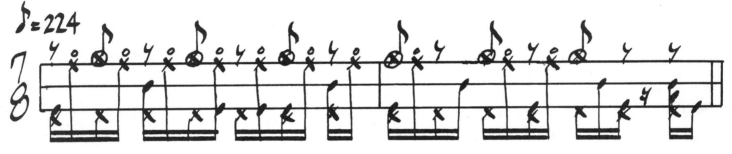

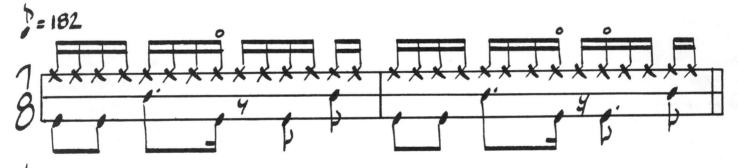

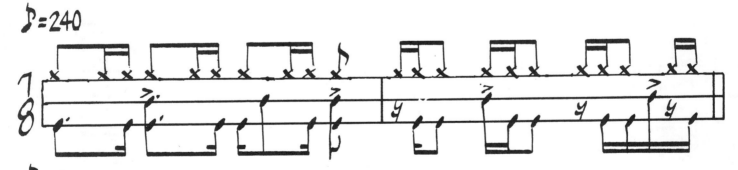

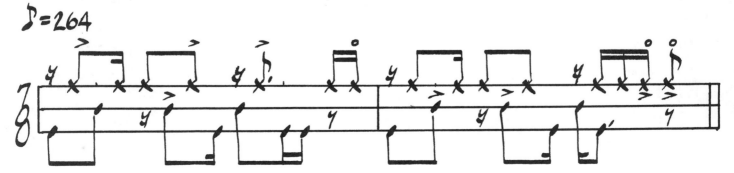

This 9/8 exercise is subdivided into one bar of 4/4 plus one-eighth note. This gives the rhythm the effect of a slightly elongated measure of 4/4 or 4½/4.

In this study, three bars of 3/8 time are pieced together to achieve the feeling created by these 9/8 patterns.

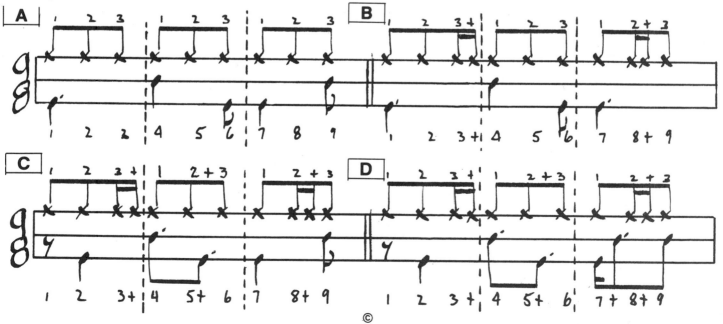

©

This study breaks down 9/8 time into a 2/4 measure followed by a 5/8 measure.

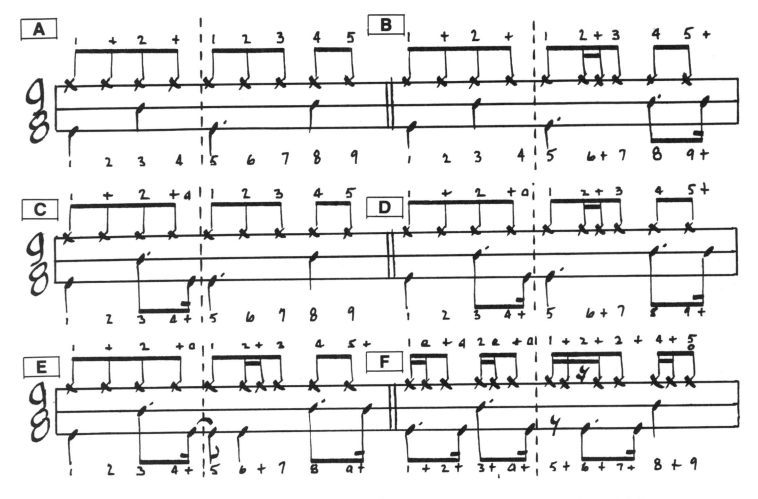

This breakdown of 9/8 begins with a 3/4 measure followed by a bar of 3/8.

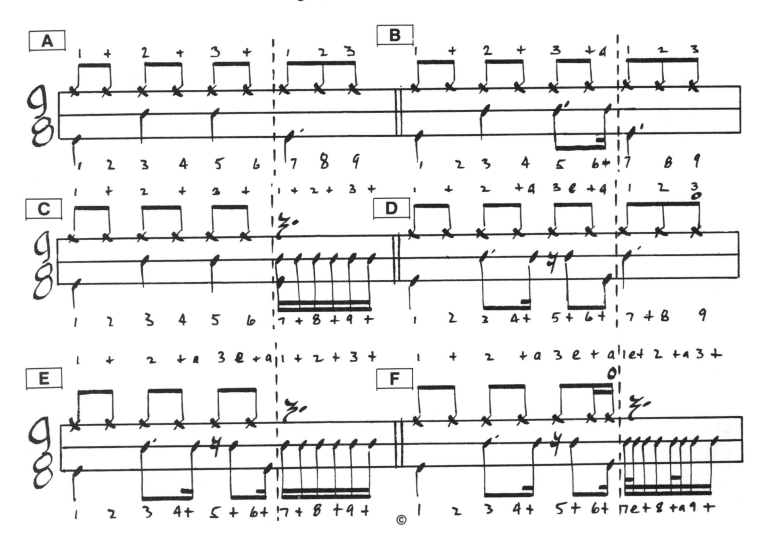

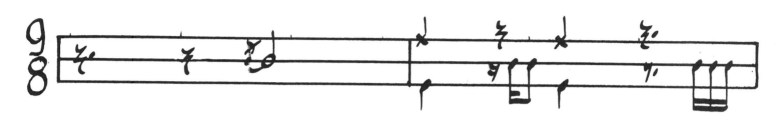

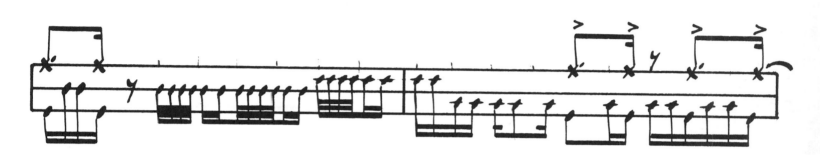

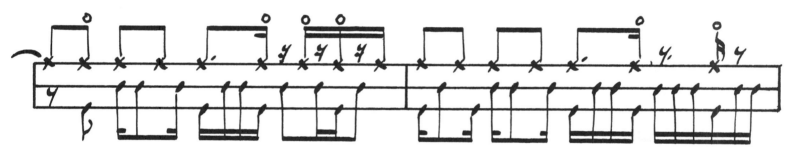

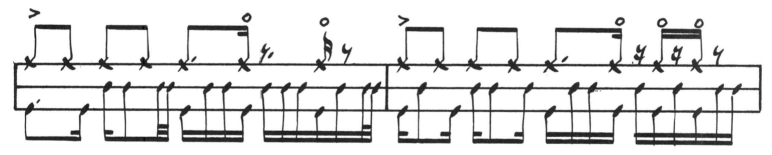

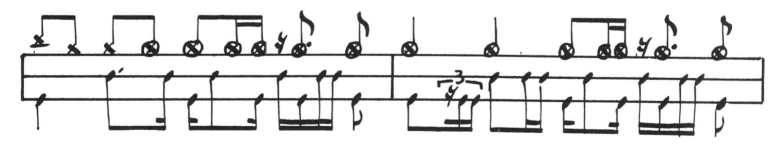

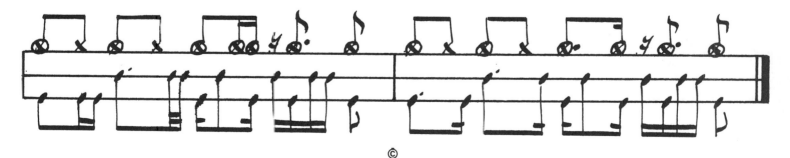

MUSICAL EXAMPLE CONTINUED...

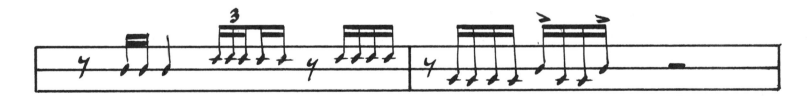

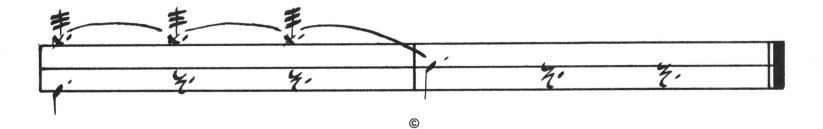

©

MUSICAL EXAMPLE NO. 6

♪ = 276

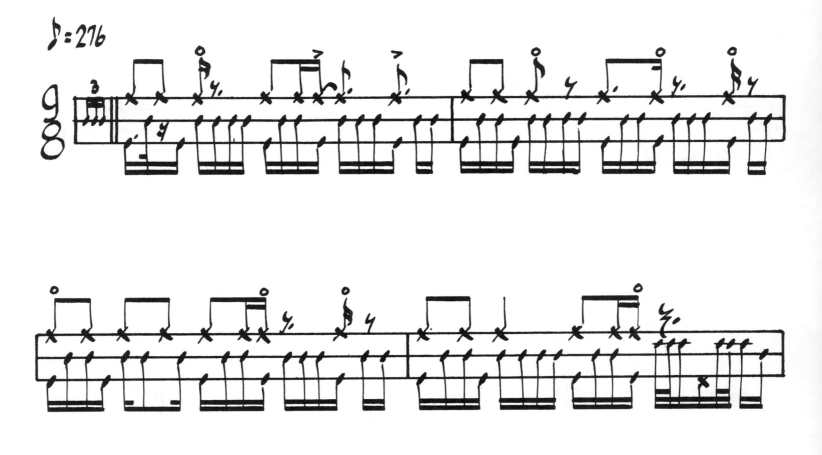

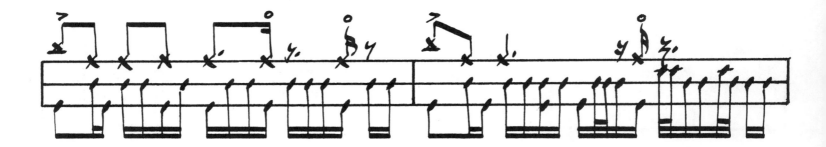

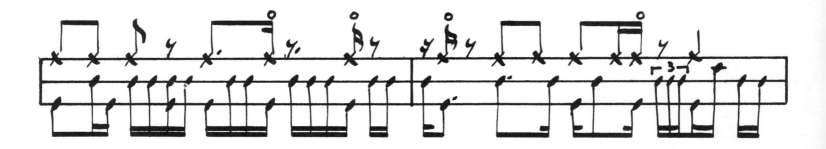

©

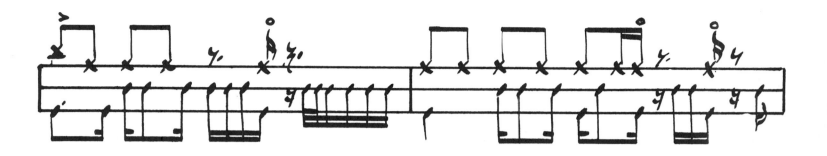

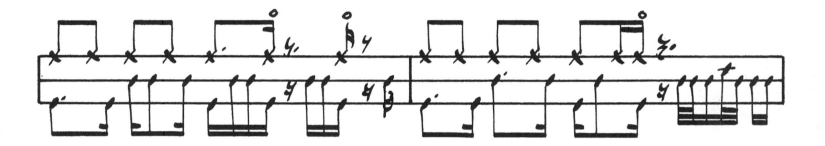

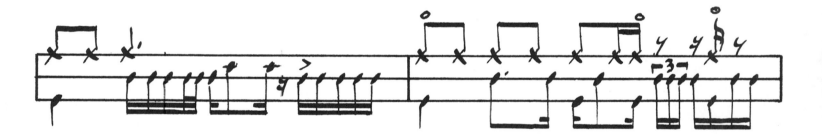

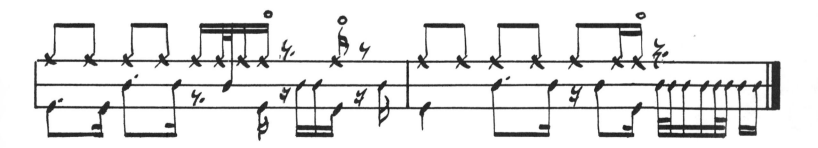

PRELIMINARY EXERCISES IN 11/8

This first 11/8 study creates the feeling of a bar of 4/4 time followed by a 3/8 measure.

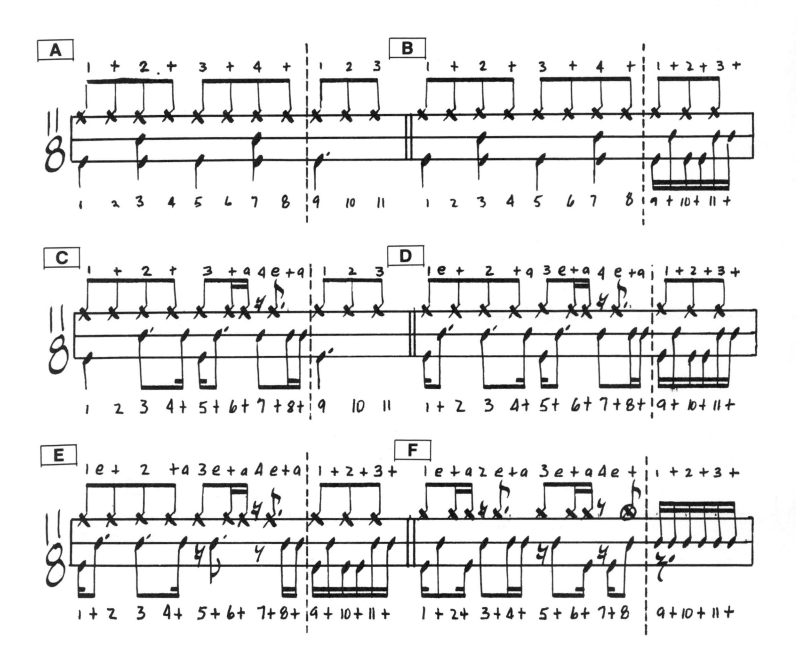

This breakdown has 11/8 described as a 3/4 measure plus a bar of 5/8.

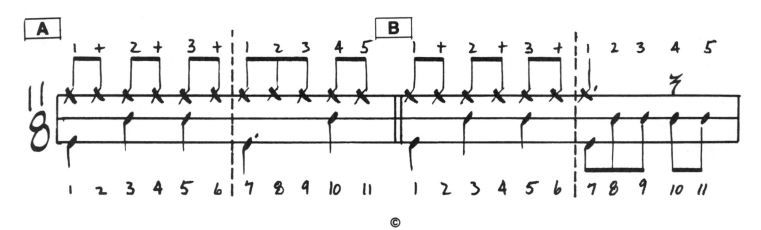

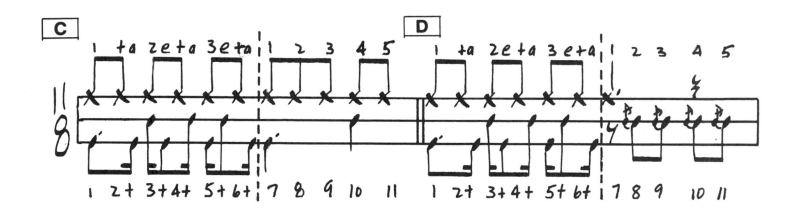

These 11/8 rhythms have the effect of a 5/8 measure followed by a bar of 6/8.

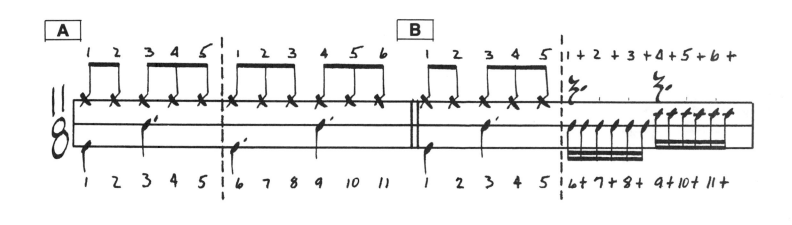

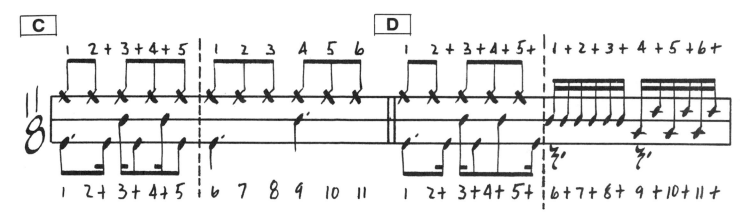

MUSICAL EXAMPLE NO. 7

MUSICAL EXAMPLE CONTINUED...

©

24

PRELIMINARY EXERCISES IN $\frac{5}{8}$

In this 5/8 study, the measure is broken down into 2/4 plus one-eighth note.

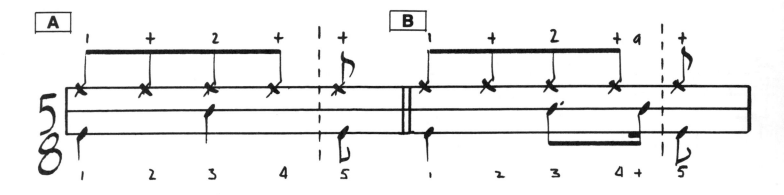

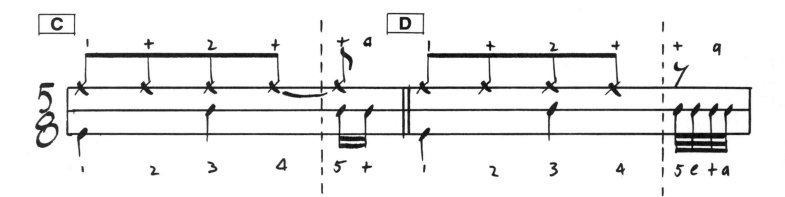

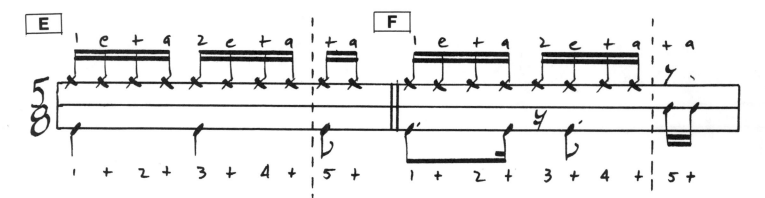

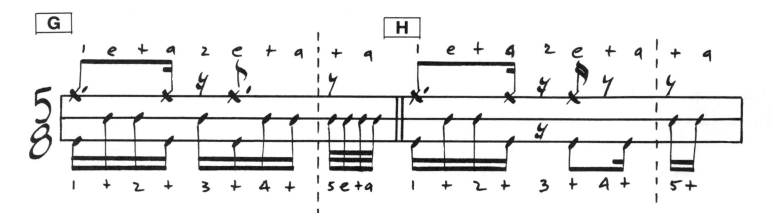

These are examples of 5/8 time broken down into 3/8 plus 2/8.

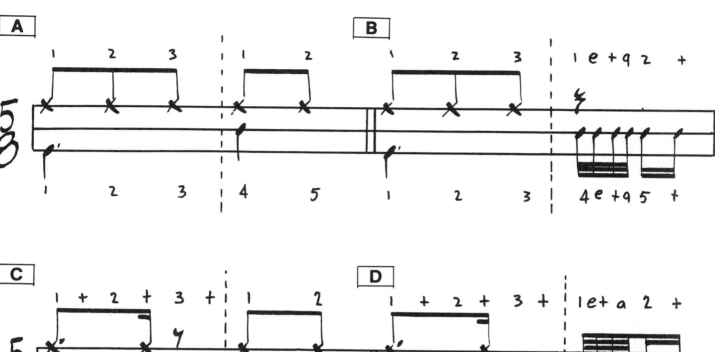

In this study, the 5/8 measure is thought of as 2/8 plus 3/8.

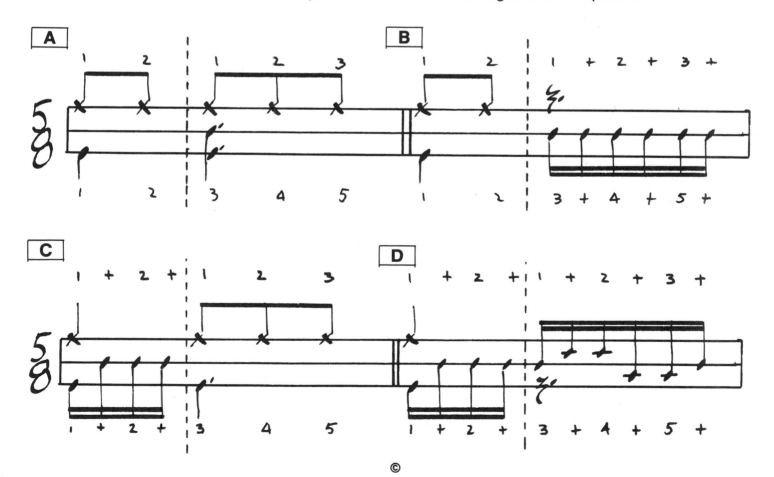

MUSICAL EXAMPLE NO. 8

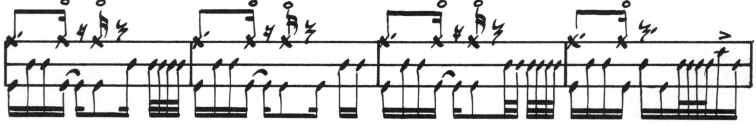

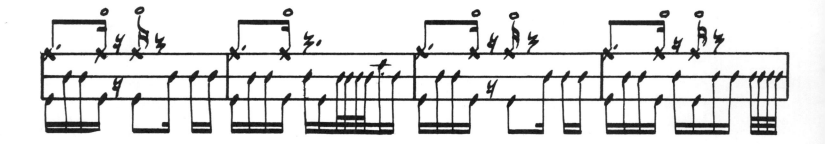

MUSICAL EXAMPLE CONTINUED...

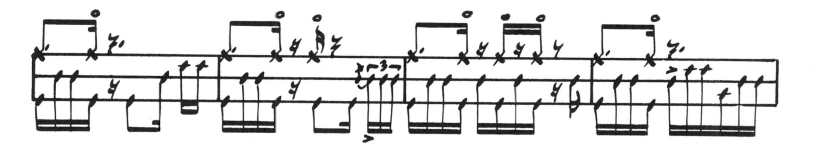

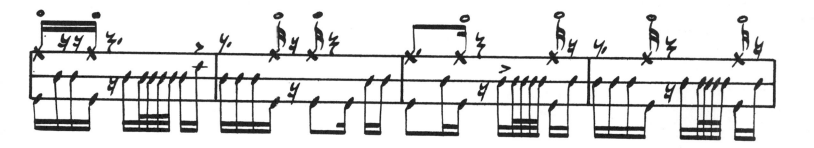

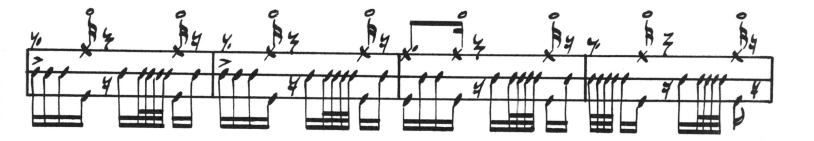

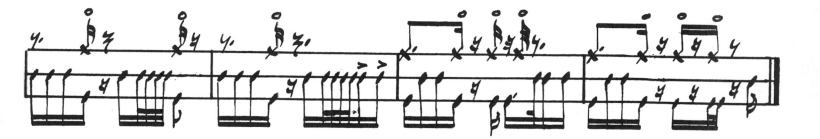

Ⓖ

PRELIMINARY EXERCISES IN 6/8

These exercises in 6/8 can be counted as 2 bars of 3/8.

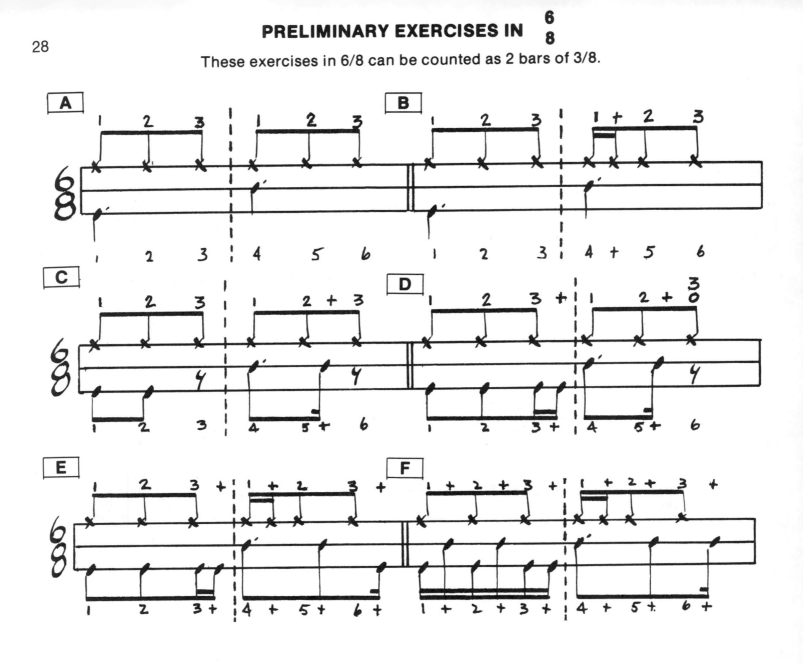

This is an example of the 6/8 clave rhythm.

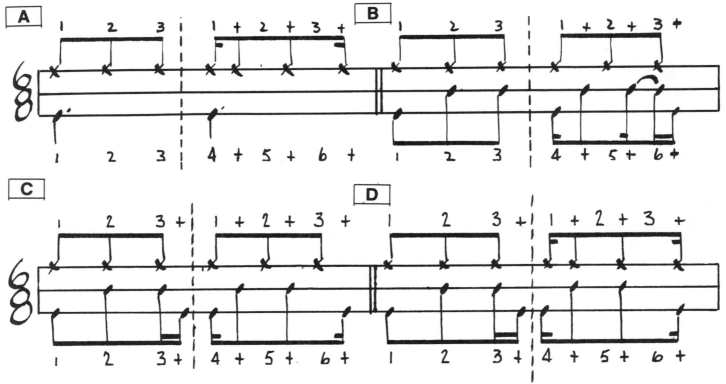

©

PRELIMINARY EXERCISE CONTINUED...

Here are some examples of 6/8 fill-ins with a 3/4 feel.

MUSICAL EXAMPLE NO. 9

♩.=84

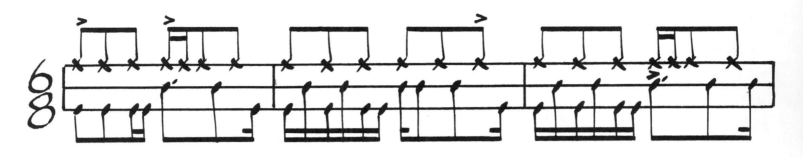

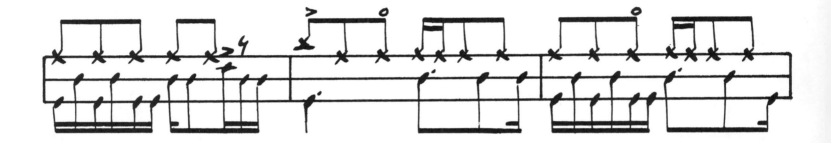

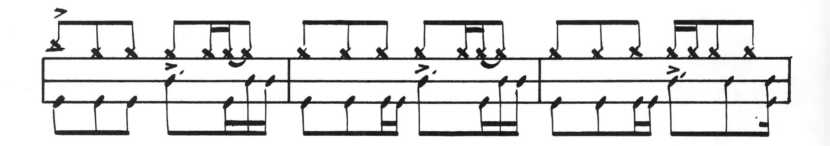

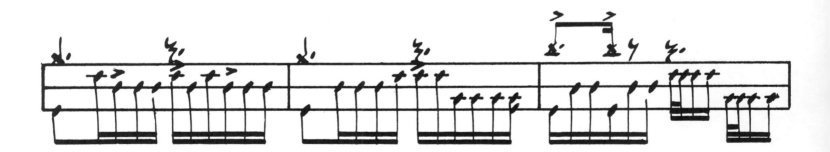

MUSICAL EXAMPLE CONTINUED...

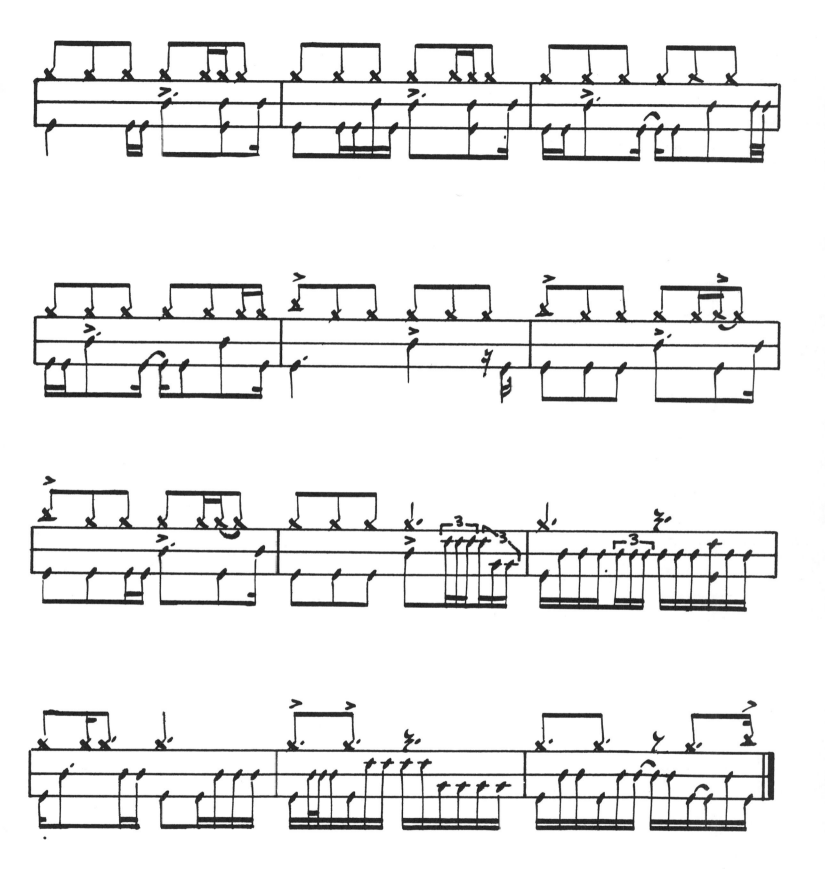

MUSICAL EXAMPLE NO. 10

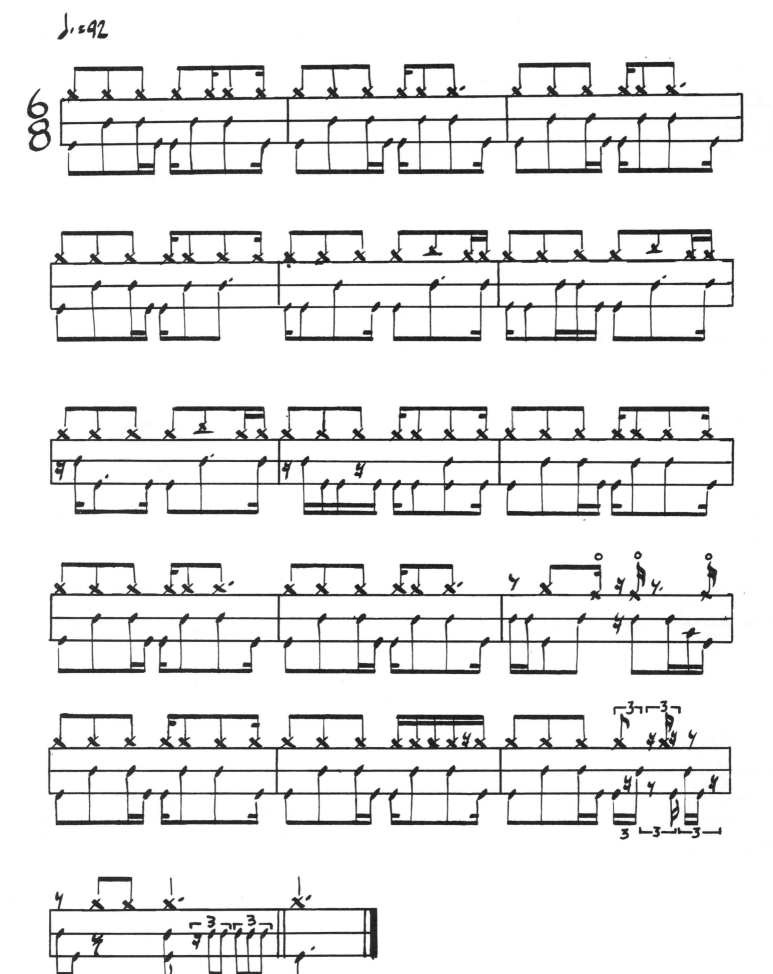

In this 19/8 exercise the 4/4 rhythm comes first it is followed by a bar of 5/8 then a bar of 6/8.

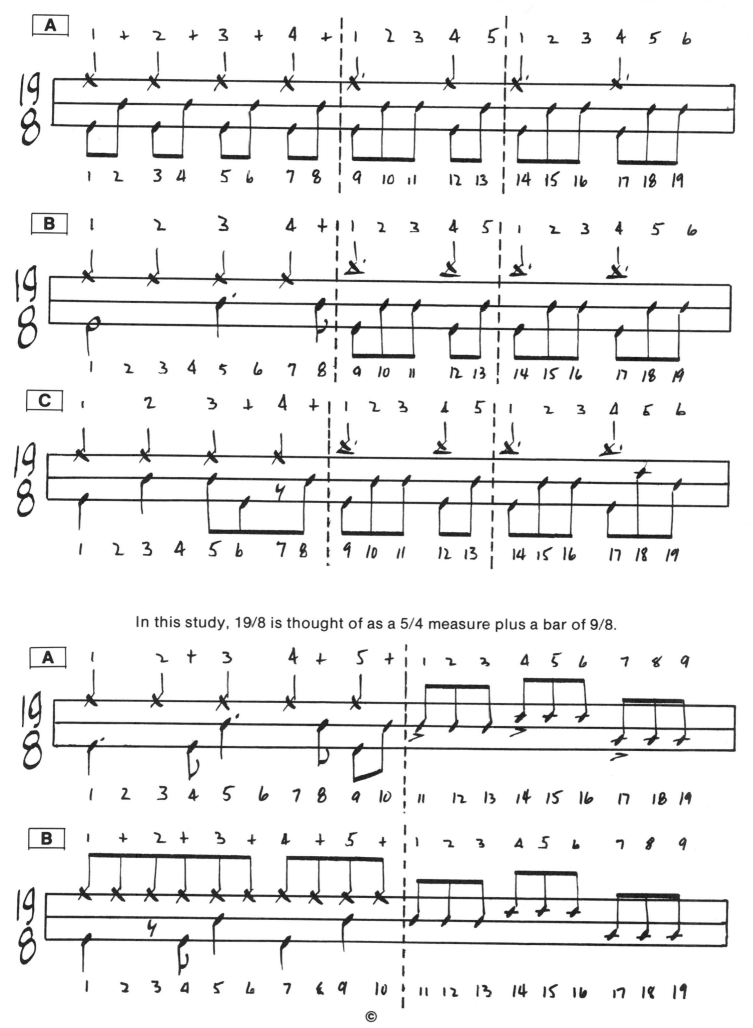

In this study, 19/8 is thought of as a 5/4 measure plus a bar of 9/8.

This 19/8 exercise is being broken down into 2 measures of 4/4 plus 3/8.

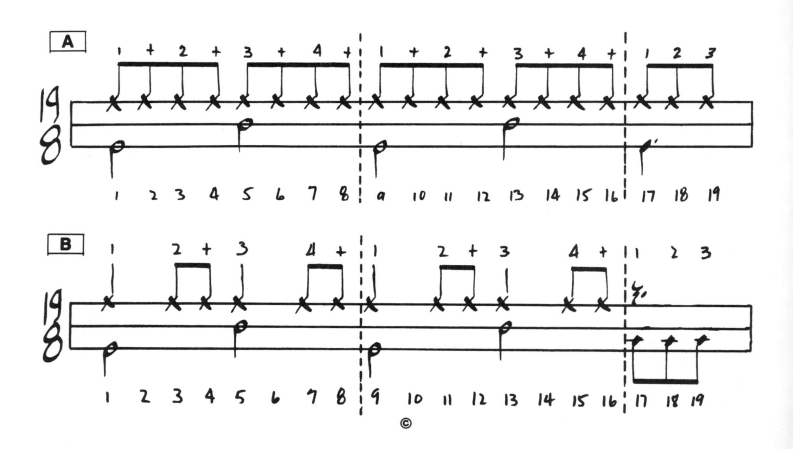

PRELIMINARY EXERCISE CONTINUED...

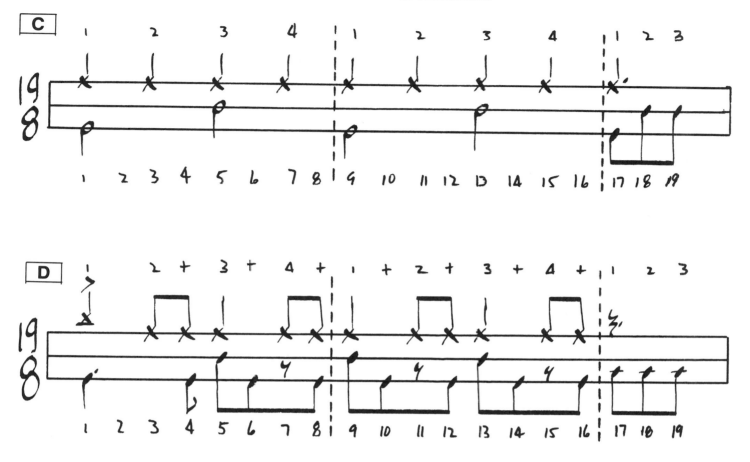

These patterns can also be thought of as 4/4 plus 3/16 or 19/16.

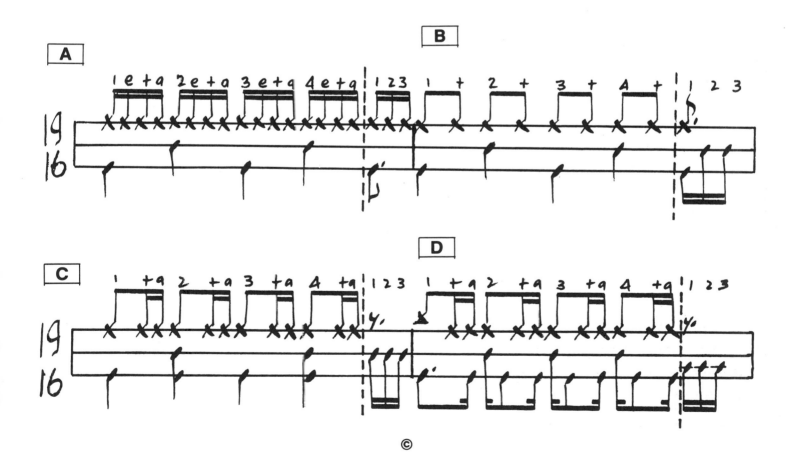

©

MUSICAL EXAMPLE NO. 11

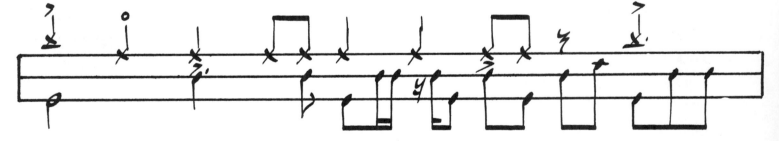

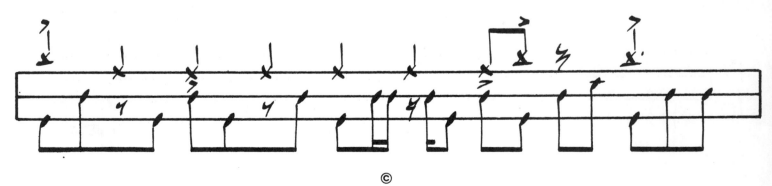

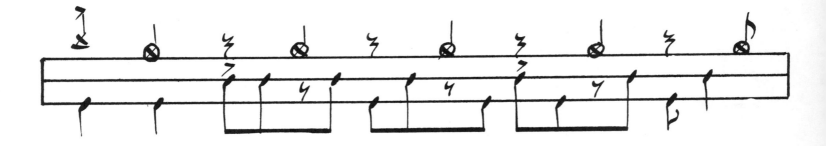

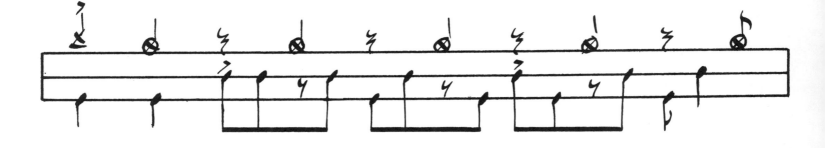

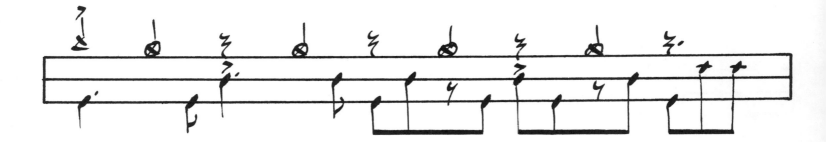

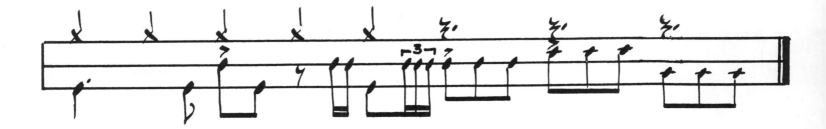

PRELIMINARY EXERCISES IN $\frac{20}{8}$

This 20/8 study is thought of as 6/4 plus 4/4.

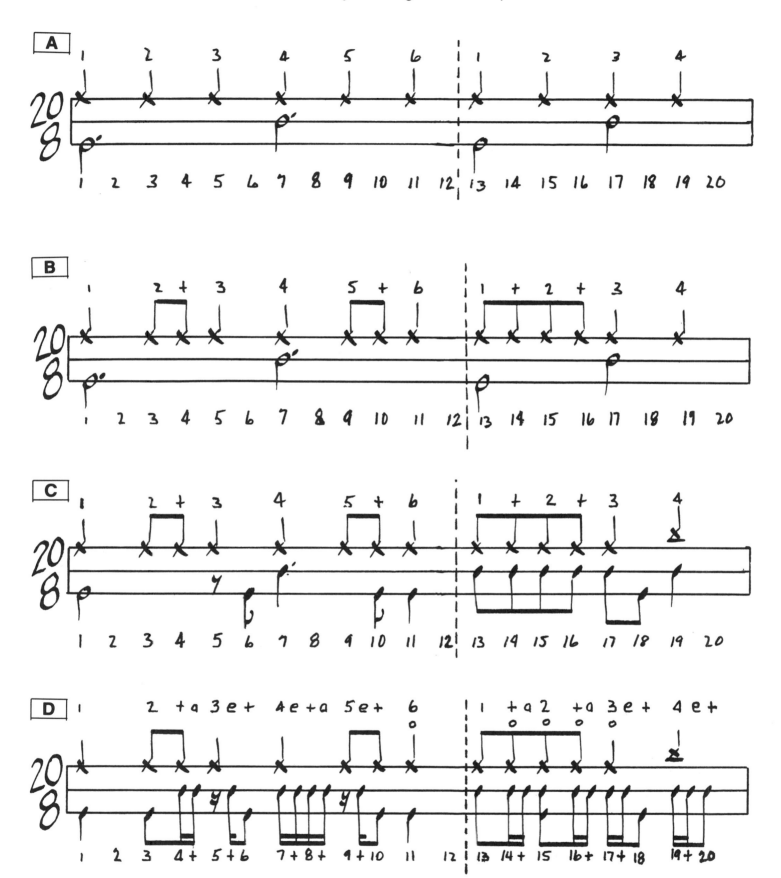

In this 20/8 exercise, there are 3 bars of 6/8 plus as bar of 2/8.

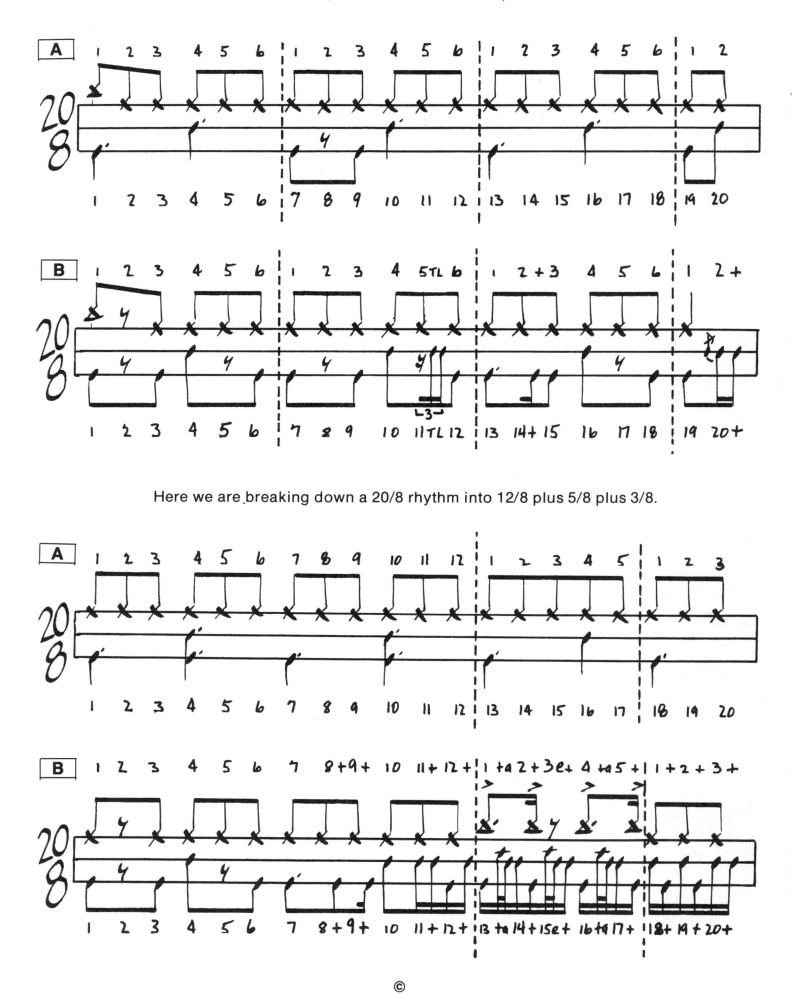

Here we are breaking down a 20/8 rhythm into 12/8 plus 5/8 plus 3/8.

MUSICAL EXAMPLE NO. 12

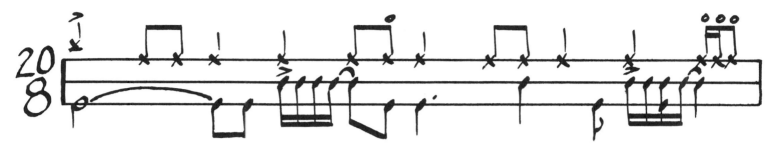

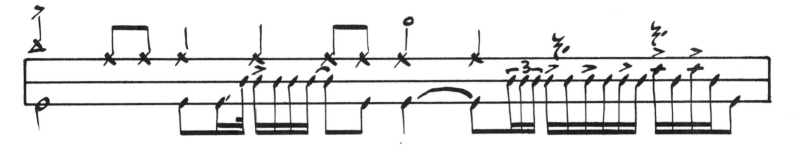

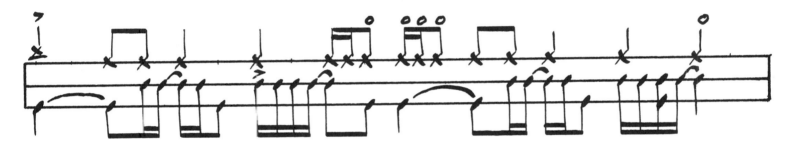

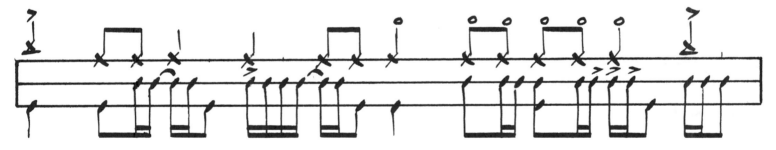

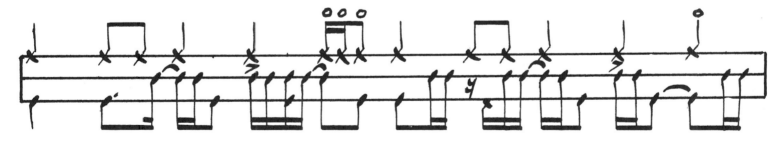

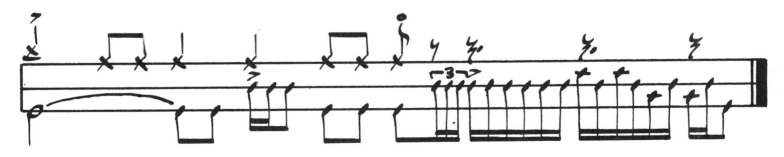

©

MUSICAL EXAMPLE NO. 13

PRELIMINARY EXERCISES IN $\frac{3}{4}$

The study of quarter note based rhythms begins with 3/4 time.

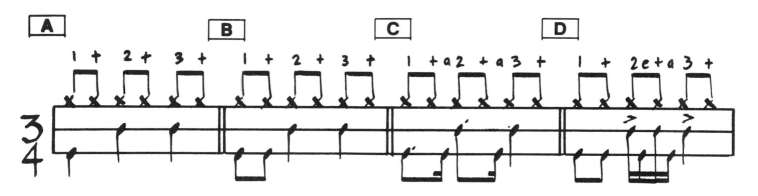

These are examples of 3/4 fill-ins with a 6/8 feel.

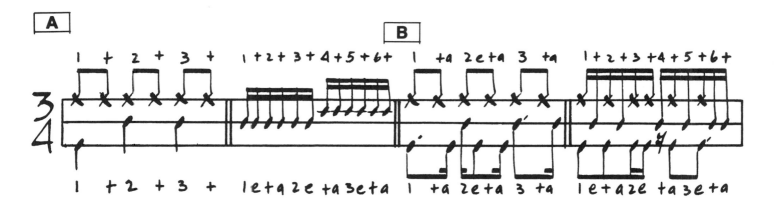

PRELIMINARY EXERCISE IN $\frac{5}{4}$

Here there is a 5/4 time subdivided into 3/4 plus 2/4.

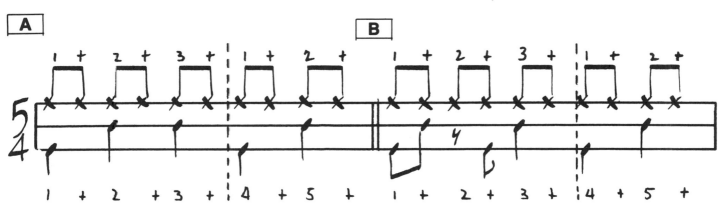

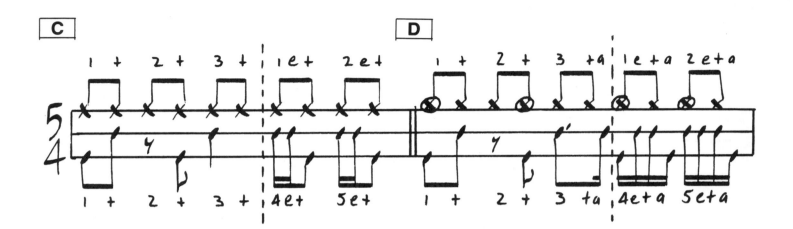

This example shows 5/4 broken down into 2/4 plus 3/4.

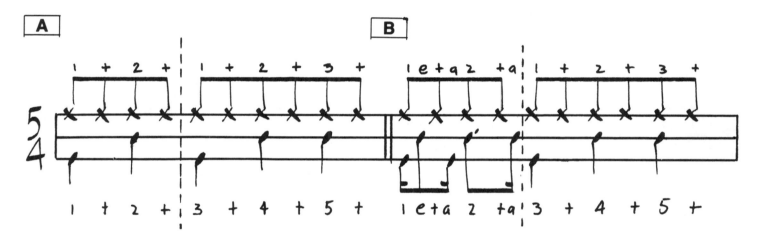

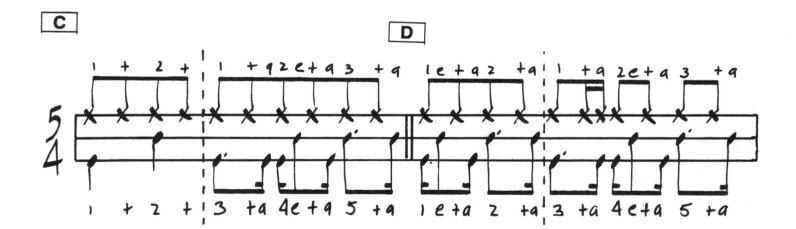

©

♩ = 120

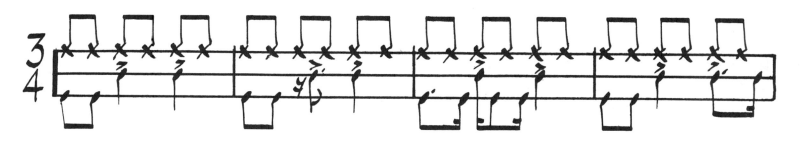

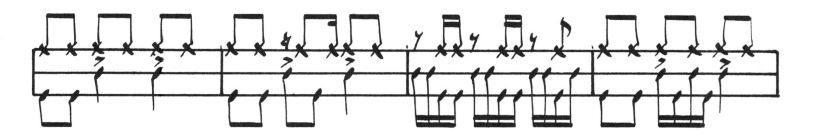

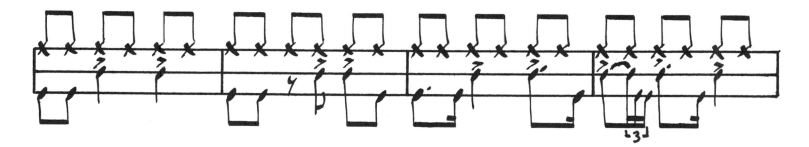

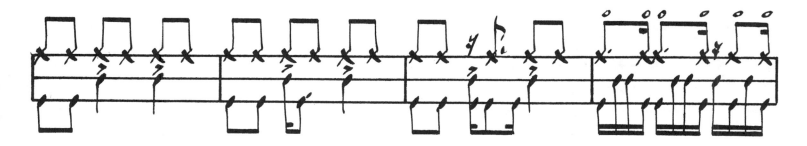

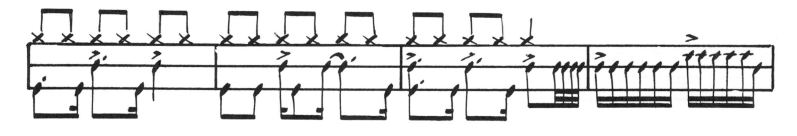

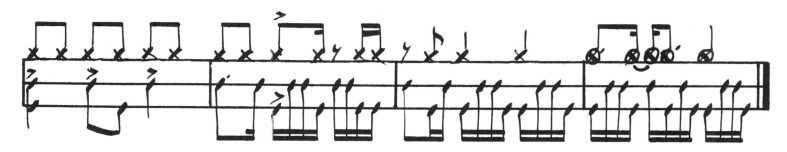

MUSICAL EXAMPLE NO. 15

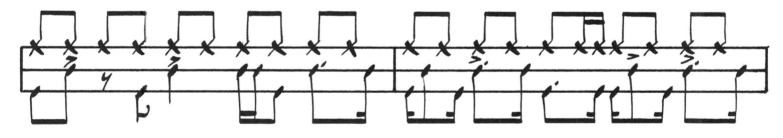

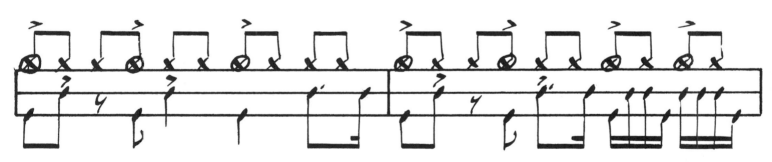

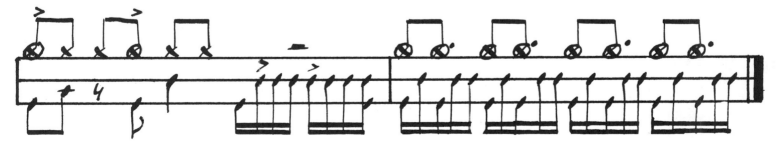

PRELIMINARY EXERCISES IN 6/4

This 6/4 study is subdivided into 4/4 plus 2/4.

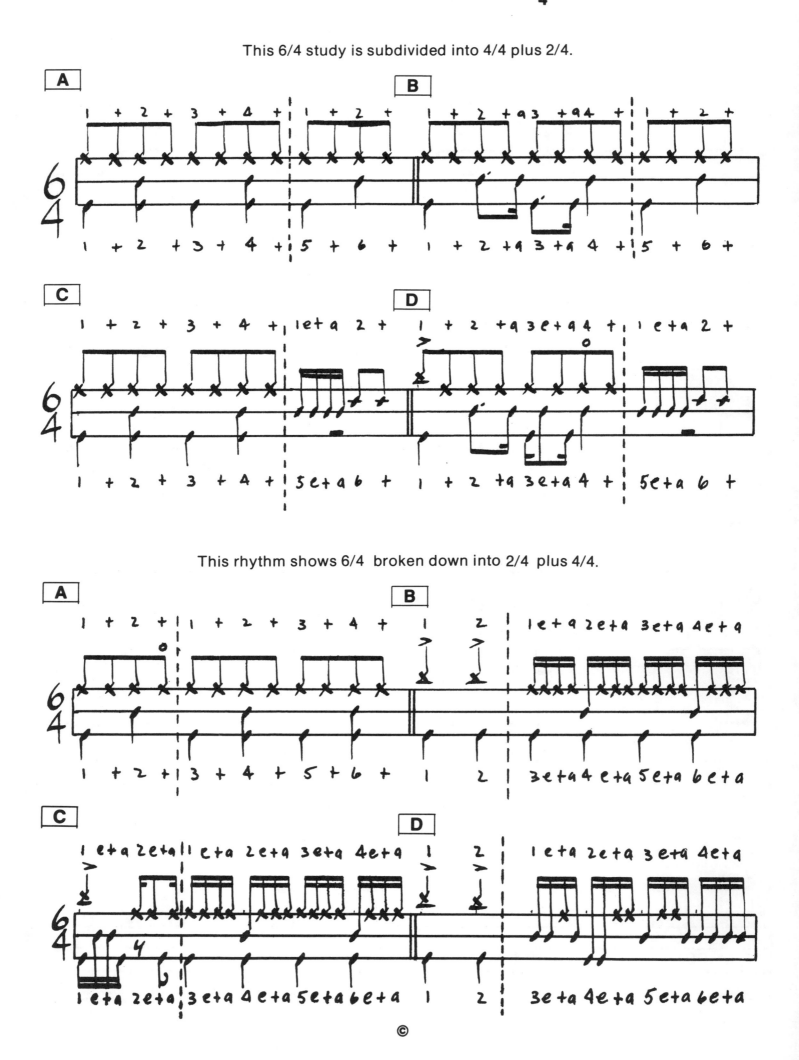

This rhythm shows 6/4 broken down into 2/4 plus 4/4.

©

Next there is 6/4 subdivided into 3/4 plus 3/4.

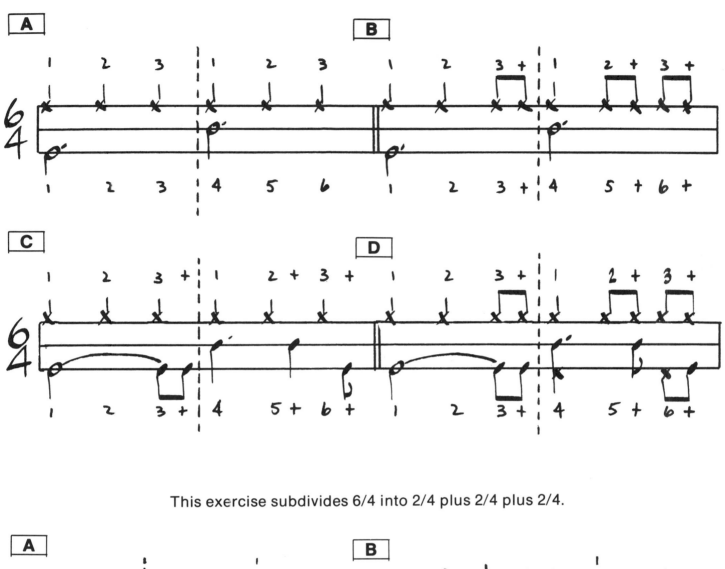

This exercise subdivides 6/4 into 2/4 plus 2/4 plus 2/4.

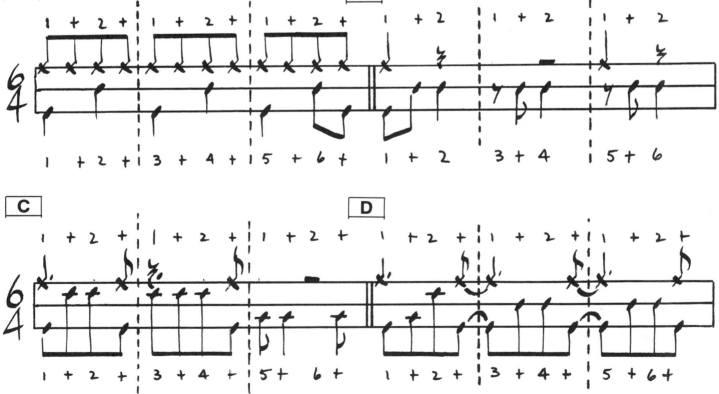

MUSICAL EXAMPLE NO. 16

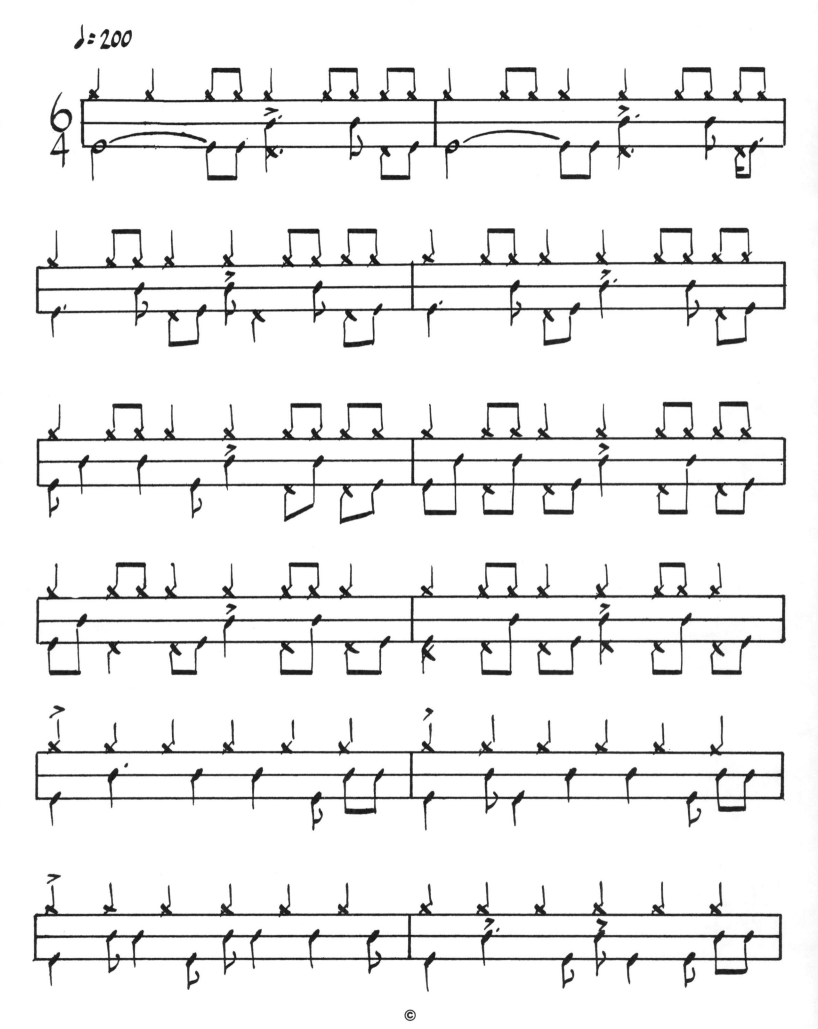

MUSICAL EXAMPLE CONTINUED...

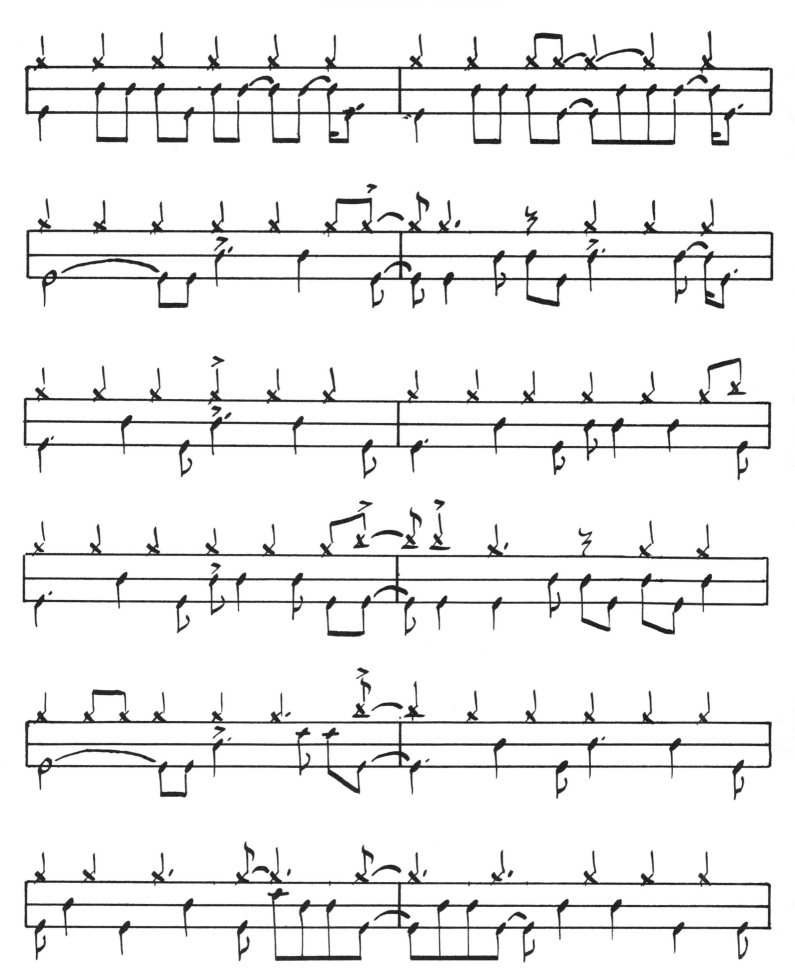

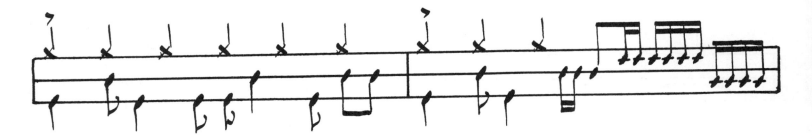

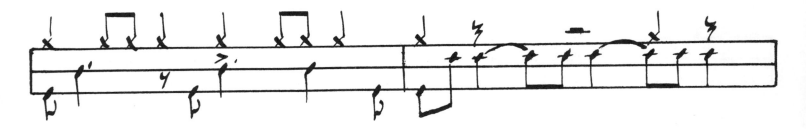

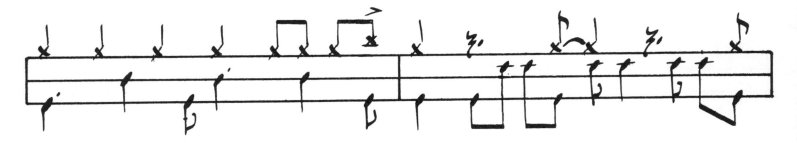

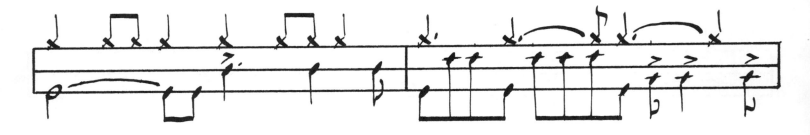

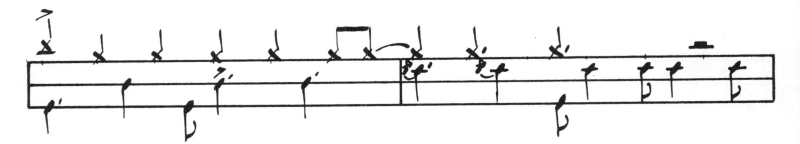

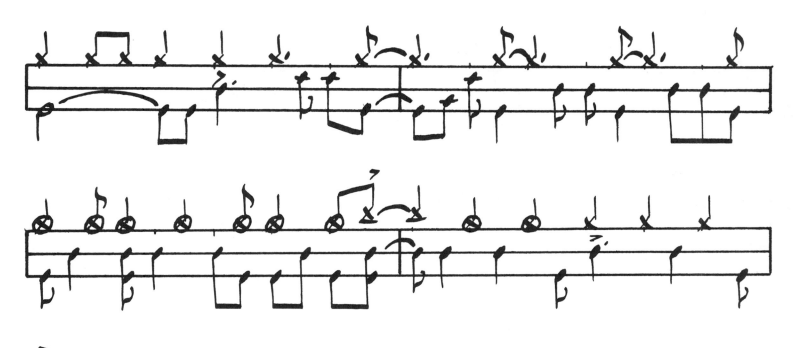

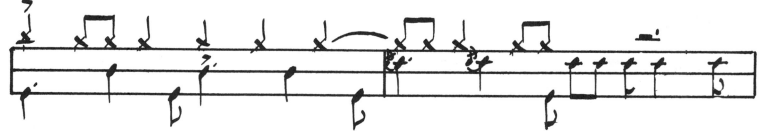

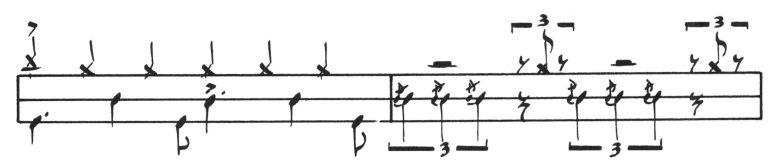

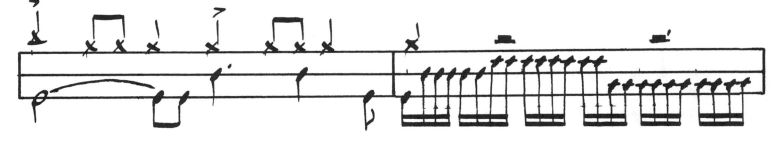

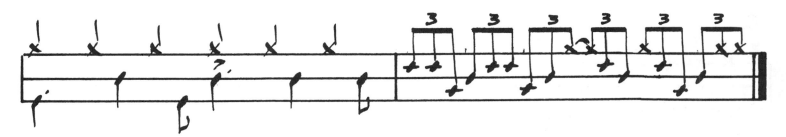

MUSICAL EXAMPLE NO. 17

♩=116

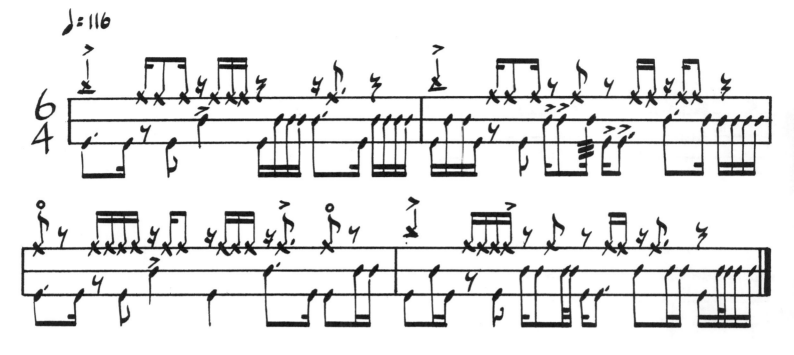

MUSICAL EXAMPLE NO. 18

♩=132

©

PRELIMINARY EXERCISES IN $\frac{7}{4}$

Here is a 7/4 study broken down into 4/4 plus 3/4.

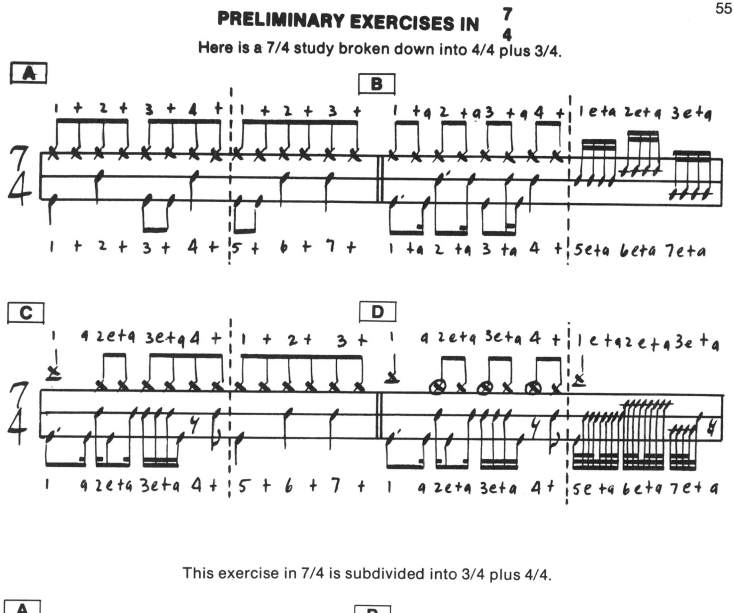

This exercise in 7/4 is subdivided into 3/4 plus 4/4.

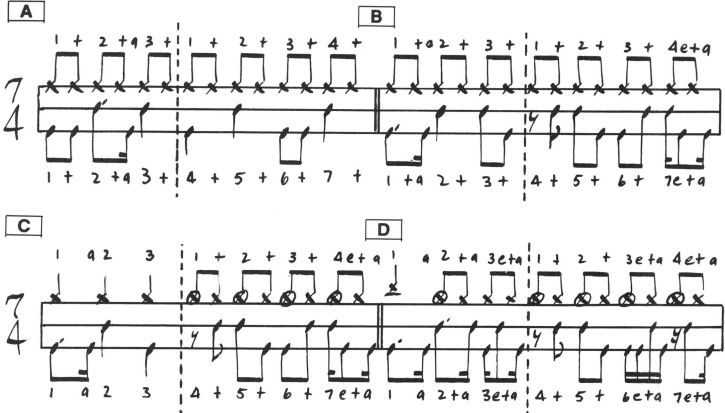

©

PRELIMINARY EXERCISE CONTINUED...

Next we have a triplet feel in 7/4 subdivided 4/4 plus 3/4.

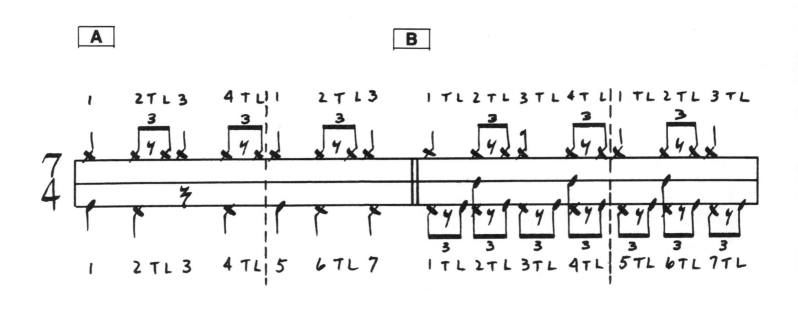

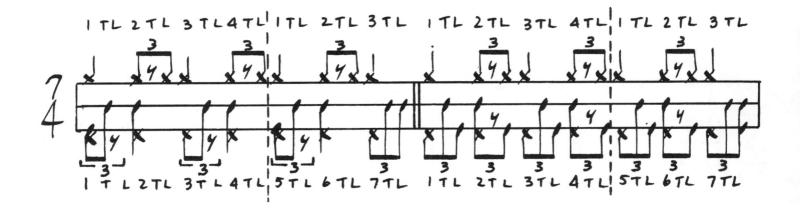

MUSICAL EXAMPLE NO. 19

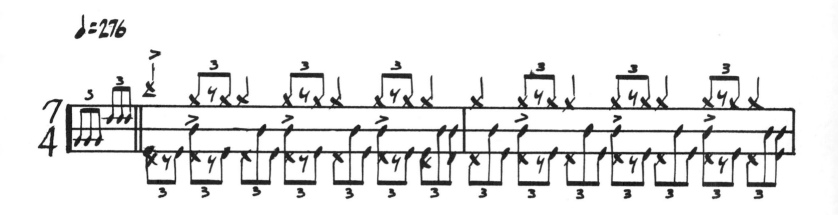

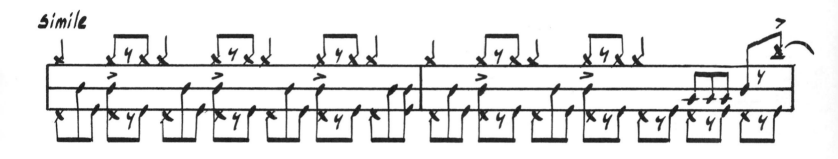

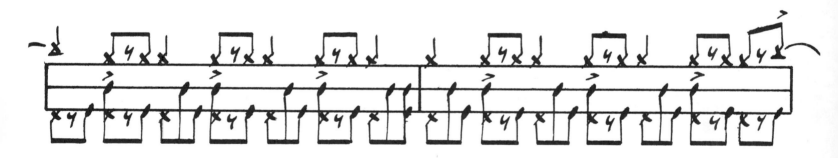

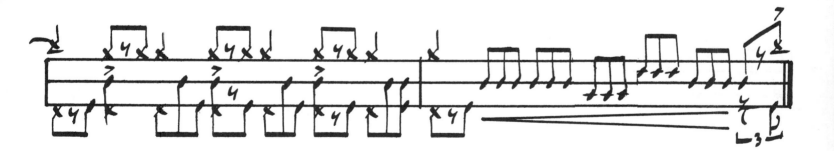

MUSICAL EXAMPLE NO. 20

♩=132

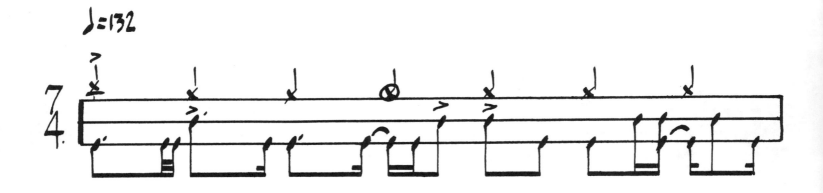

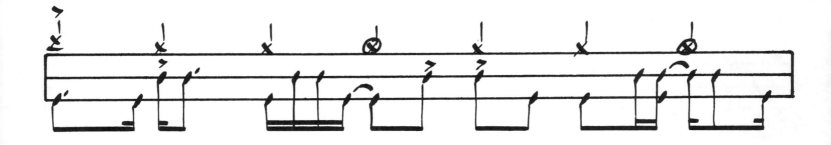

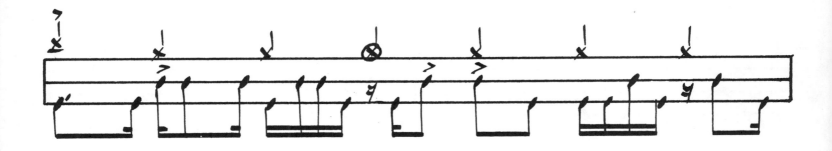

©

MUSICAL EXAMPLE CONTINUED...

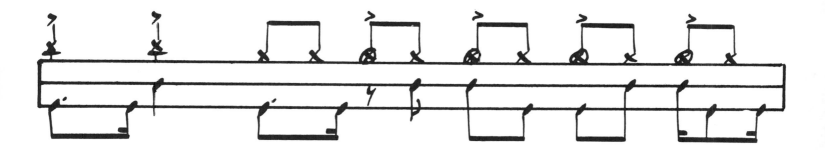

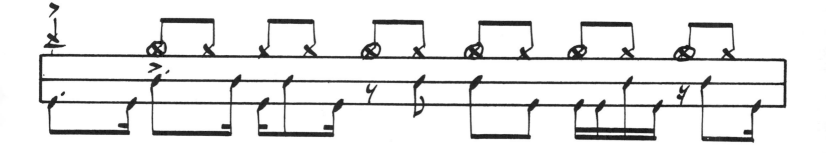

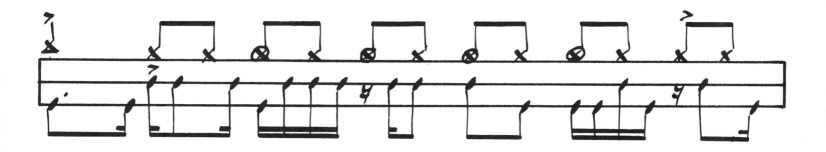

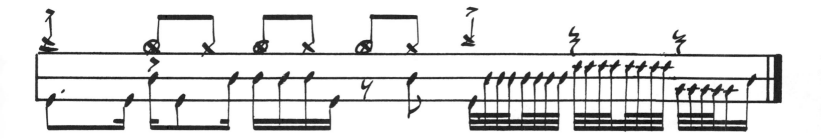

©

PRELIMINARY EXERCISES IN $\frac{4}{4} + \frac{6}{8}$

Here there is an example of going from 4/4 to 6/8 which can also be thought of as 14/8.

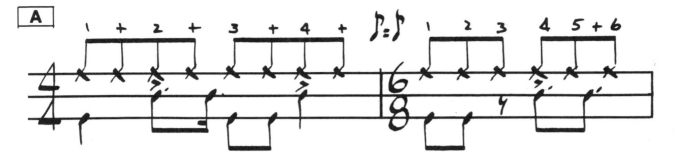

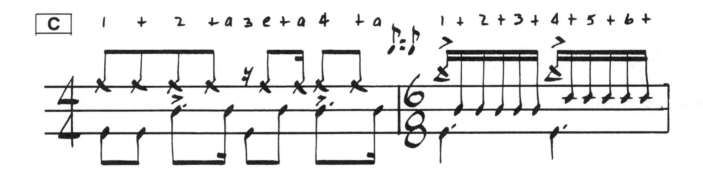

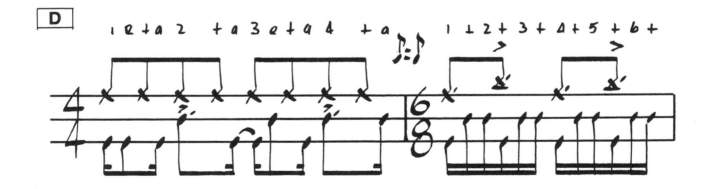

PRELIMINARY EXERCISES IN $\frac{7}{8} + \frac{4}{4}$

This musical breakdown shows the technique of changing meter from 7/8 to 4/4. This can also be thought of as 15/8.

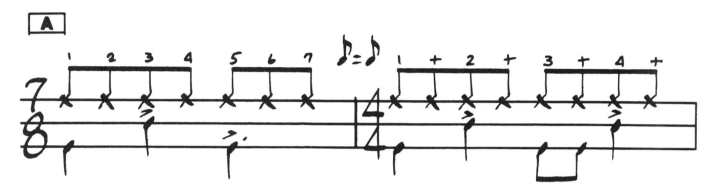

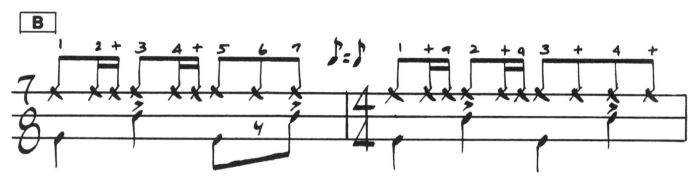

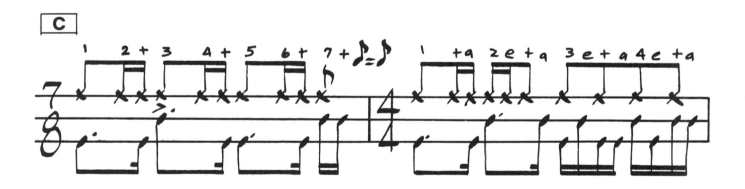

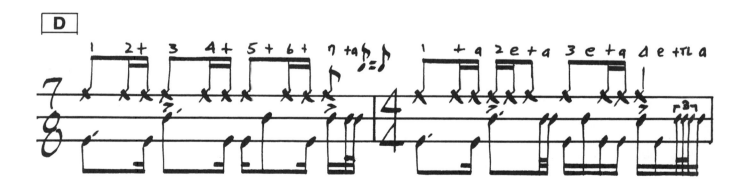

MUSICAL EXAMPLE NO. 22

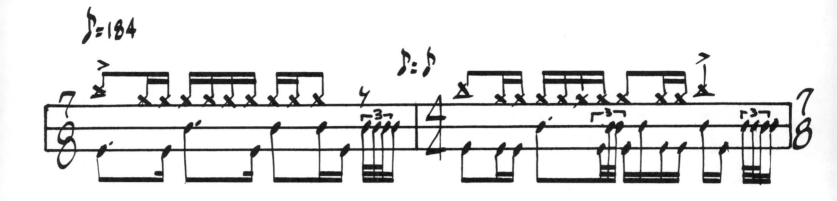

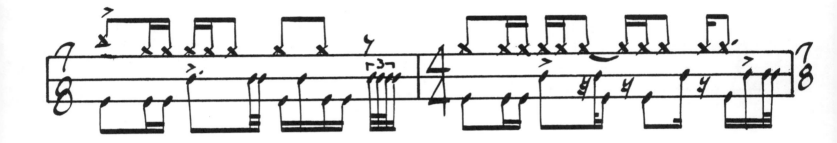

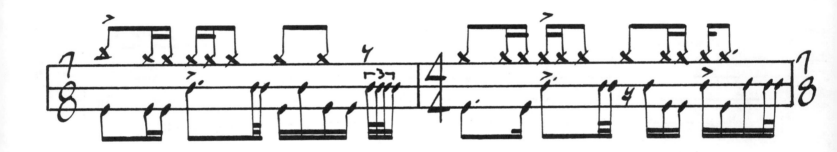

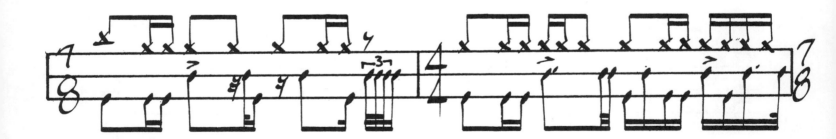

MUSICAL EXAMPLE CONTINUED...

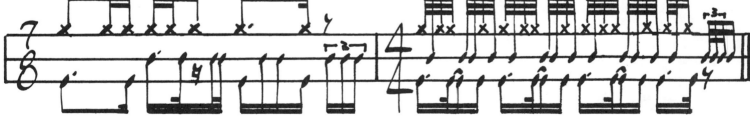

PHRASING ODD METERS WITHIN A 4/4 TIME STRUCTURE

Once you are comfortable playing in the time signatures presented in this text you may then begin to apply the rhythms to 4/4. Many creative drummers play phrases in odd meters within the structure of a 4/4 tune. This rhythmic device creates interesting counter-rhythms. The technique, which can be thought of as playing meter within meter*, is played across the bar line. Do not confuse this technique with polyrhythm*. Discretion and taste are paramount when initiating this concept into your playing.

This first study presents a 4/4 rhythm of 2 measures in length. It is then broken down into several odd groupings which add up to 8 quarter notes. The basic rhythm is kept intact, however the snare drum-bass drum combinations have been voiced differently to better illustrate the different phrasings.

(Editor's Note)   *See Art of Modern Jazz Drumming by Jack DeJohnette and Charlie Perry.

**See Musicians Guide to Polyrhythms by Peter Magadini Vol. I, II.

©

These are selected combinations of odd meters that blend particularly well together to complete 8 quarter notes (2 bars of 4/4).

The same rhythms are written over again 4/4 time to help you understand how the patterns conform to a 4/4 time structure.

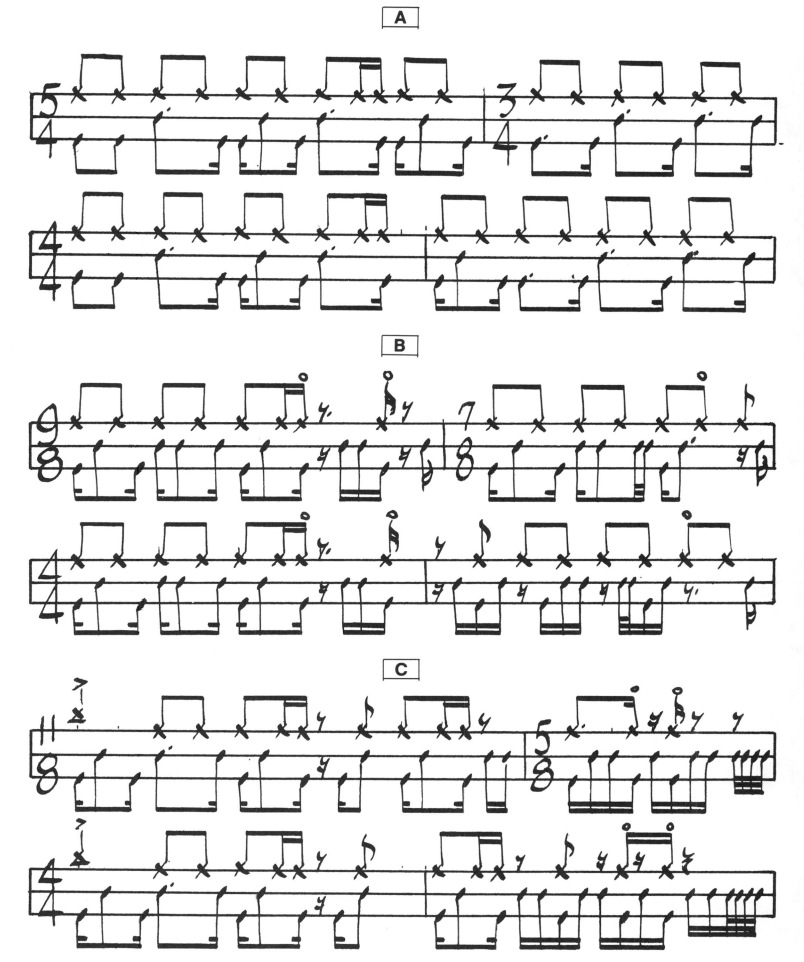

MUSICAL EXAMPLE NO. 23

Here we have a 4 bar pattern applying the concept of meter within meter in the 3rd and 4th measure.

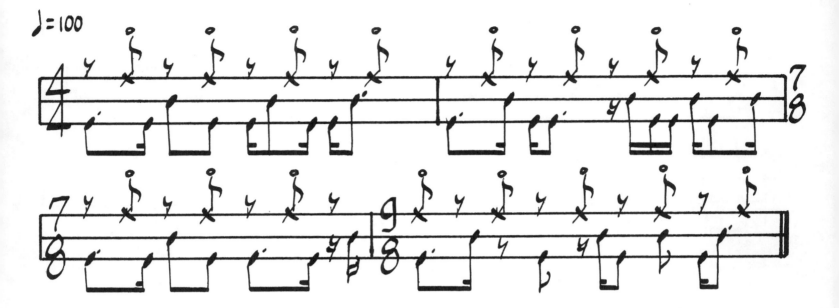

MUSICAL EXAMPLE NO. 24

This pattern sounds identical to the previous example however it is written completely in 4/4.

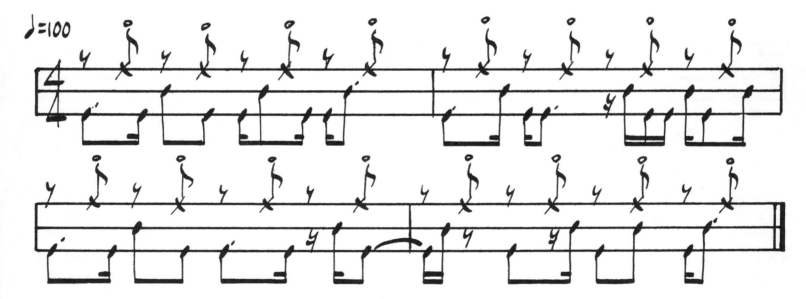

MUSICAL EXAMPLE NO. 25

Here we have an 8 bar musical example in 4/4. Learn this example first in order to prepare yourself to understand how these same rhythms are phrased differently in the next study.

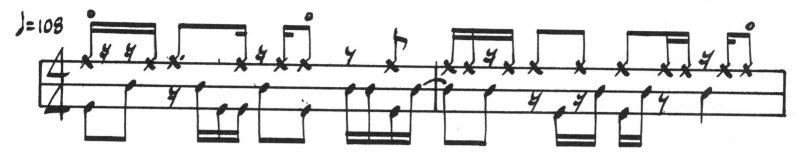

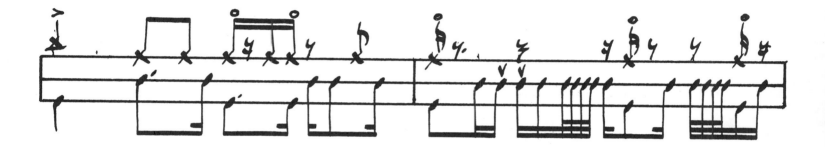

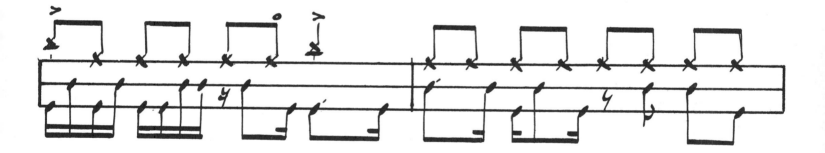

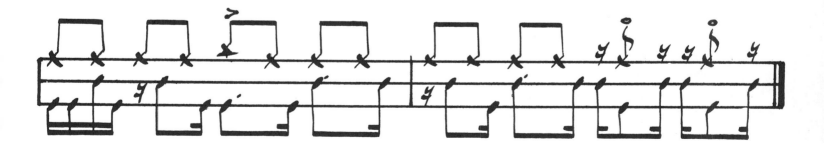

©

MUSICAL EXAMPLE NO. 26

This is one other way that you could phrase Musical Example No. 25 using the concept of phrasing odd meters within a 4/4 time structure. Just as we speak, we could say the same phrase and use a different inflection to change its significance. Rhythms can be dealt with in the same manner. There are endless possibilities for phrasing these rhythms. It is suggested that you continually experiment until ideas begin to appear naturally in your playing.

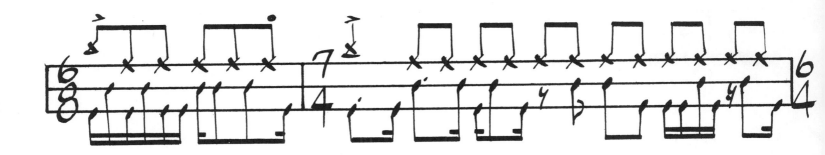

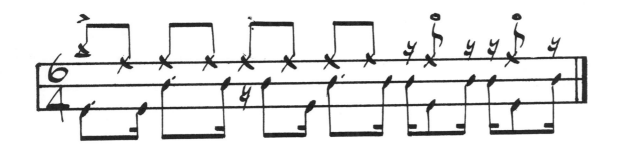

AMETRIC STUDIES

In ametric playing the rhythms have no metric base. Bar lines are purposely eliminated. The drummer maintains a strong sense of time while allowing his ideas to flow without concern for time signature. In a musical performance context these rhythms would progress according to what musical stimuli the drummer is responding to and/or what he's trying to initiate himself rather than strict time keeping patterns.

MUSICAL EXAMPLE NO. 27

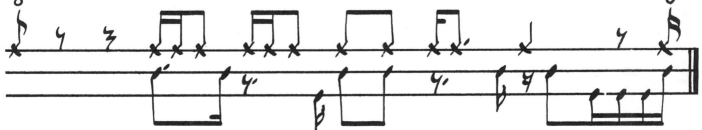

MUSICAL EXAMPLE NO. 28

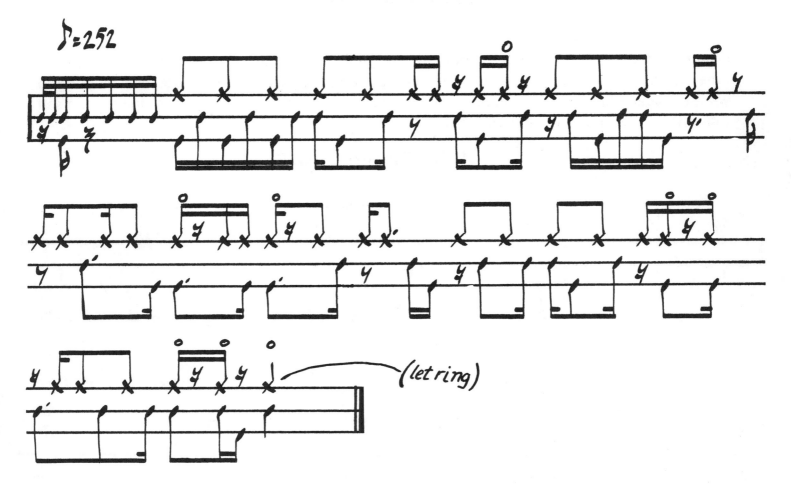

MUSICAL EXAMPLE NO. 29

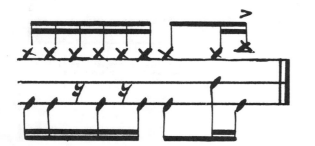

MUSICAL EXAMPLE NO. 30

♪=208

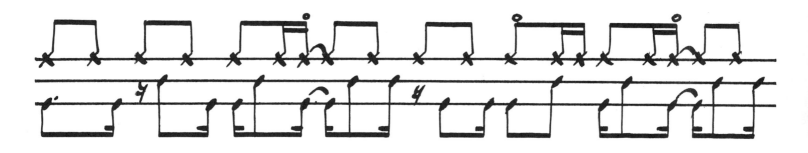

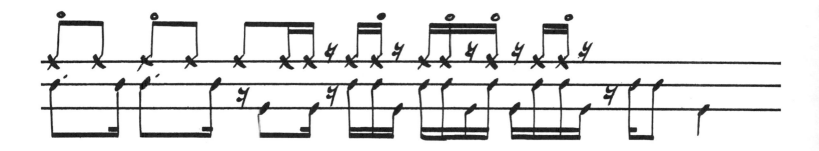

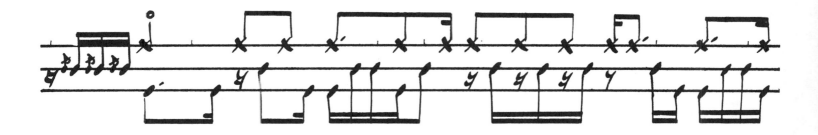

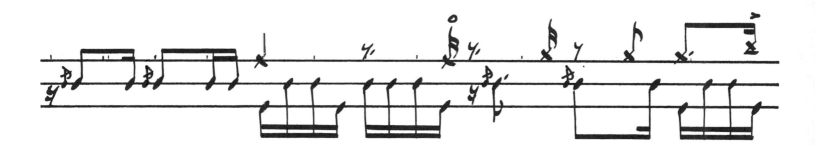

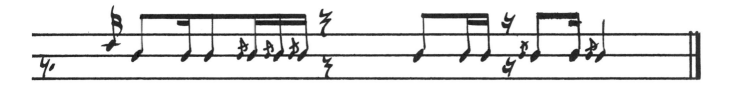

FINE